Ludic Dreaming is provocative and adventurous in thought and style, offering a fresh approach to the thinking of sound, and a whimsical, highly productive, excursion from the field.

—*Frances Dyson, Emeritus Professor in Cinema and Digital Media University of California, Davis, USA*

Dreams do not distort reality, so much as they are the reality of that distortion. *Ludic Dreaming* puts dreams in contact with electronic sounds, and digital devices more generally, in order to trace out the exotic topology of our post-everything society.

—*Steven Shaviro, DeRoy Professor of English Wayne State University, USA*

This book is a piece of sound writing. Blurring the boundaries between dream, vision and physics, it stretches the reader's imagination into playful and oneiric realms of sonic materiality. A gift.

— *Deborah A. Kapchan, Associate Professor of Performance Studies New York University USA*

If contemporary networked capitalism is built on promissory hallucinations to which we wake in fright, then *Ludic Dreaming* is both sonic boom and boon for an altogether different reverie. Its essays hum with the aural ludicrousness of technocultural phenomena – from black holes that emit B-flat frequencies to new generation ear buds that purport to (almost) playback the voice inside our heads. But in ludically tuning in to our nightmarish technologies, Cecchetto, Couroux, Hiebert and Priest [or The Occulture] concurrently compose a delirious counter-counterpoint accompaniment. And herein lies the remarkable and highly original contribution of this book to cultural theory, media and sound studies, and speculative thought. Affording listening a speculative creativity rather than mere receptive functionality, *Ludic Dreaming* performs an 'elsewhere' listening; a sounding of novel spectra into existence. You will never want to wake up from *Ludic Dreaming*!

—*Anna Munster, Associate Professor, Art and Design University of New South Wales, Australia*

LUDIC DREAMING

LUDIC DREAMING

How to Listen Away from Contemporary Technoculture

BY
THE OCCULTURE:
DAVID CECCHETTO
MARC COUROUX
TED HIEBERT
ELDRITCH PRIEST

Bloomsbury Academic
An imprint of Bloomsbury Publishing Inc

B L O O M S B U R Y
NEW YORK · LONDON · OXFORD · NEW DELHI · SYDNEY

Bloomsbury Academic
An imprint of Bloomsbury Publishing Inc

1385 Broadway
New York
NY 10018
USA

50 Bedford Square
London
WC1B 3DP
UK

www.bloomsbury.com

BLOOMSBURY and the Diana logo are trademarks of Bloomsbury Publishing Plc

First published 2017

© David Cecchetto, Marc Couroux, Ted Hiebert, Eldritch Priest, 2017

All rights reserved. No part of this publication may be reproduced or transmitted in any form or by any means, electronic or mechanical, including photocopying, recording, or any information storage or retrieval system, without prior permission in writing from the publishers.

No responsibility for loss caused to any individual or organization acting on or refraining from action as a result of the material in this publication can be accepted by Bloomsbury or the author.

Library of Congress Cataloging-in-Publication Data
A catalog record for this book is available from the Library of Congress

ISBN: HB: 978-1-5013-2079-8
PB: 978-1-5013-2080-4
ePub: 978-1-5013-2082-8
ePDF: 978-1-5013-2081-1

Cover design by Daniel Benneworth-Gray

Typeset by Integra Software Services Pvt. Ltd.

CONTENTS

Acknowledgments viii

Introduction 1

1 Auralneiricizing Time (Listening Away) 17
2 Nietzsche in B-flat: Attuning to the 'pataphysics of data 31
3 Absolute Ventriloquy (or, Earing the Senses) 45
4 Psycho(tic)acoustics 57
5 The sound of both ears oozing: Chasms, collapses, and phono-digital networks 81
6 Motivational dreamers and the 'pataphysics of exploding heads 95
7 Imaginary magnitudes and the anoriginal hypocrisy that vanishes in the meantime 109
8 We are Lesion 121

Conclusion 141

Notes 145
Index 156

ACKNOWLEDGMENTS

We're grateful to Bloomsbury for following our dreams with this project, and to Laura Banducci, Daniel Benneworth-Gray, Sarah Blake, Michelle Chen, Ally-Jane Grossan, and Patience Moll for their informed, flexible, and enthusiastic support. The Occulture exists in part as a node of the generous and lively community that has coalesced around the Tuning Speculation conferences and workshops, and many of the ideas in this book were amplified, tuned, and sometimes undermined by the fantastic—fantastic!—folks who commune with us there.

This research was supported by the Social Sciences and Humanities Research Council of Canada.

Introduction

*Fidelity is not something absolute but something
dreamed, sensed, and felt.*[1]

There has never been a night when we dreamed we were writing an Introduction. Why? Because it isn't altogether clear whether the much-maligned pronoun we can really be dreamed. After all, doesn't the singular nature of dreams pose a challenge to the kind of participatory or collaborative action that would pluralize their visions? But then again, the opposite can be true. That is, dreaming can also be understood as a method—*the* method—for thinking the multiplicity of the singular. If dreaming is anything at all, it's that it always amounts to more than any one thing. Thus, if we had dreamed of writing an Introduction, we might have dreamed the singular plurality of the questions that are taken up (or down, or around... what is the oneiric topology of taking questions?) in this book: Why, when Nietzsche went mad, did he sit at a piano for hours playing the same note over and over again? What is it to listen with mud oozing out of your ears? Do cargo cults have anything to do with musical repetition? How can a talking horse tell us that irony isn't dead?

Ludic Dreaming approaches these questions and others like them through a series of quasi-analytical essays that take the humor, (il)logic, and gibberish of dreaming as practical methods for thinking and listening away from contemporary culture's compulsive need to make itself legible, sharable, meaningful, and "real." As such, throughout this book we seek a poetical rather than empirical—or, more accurately, a poetically empirical—resolution of a world that, let's face it, has nothing but mediations to show for itself.

In a decidedly playful way, *Ludic Dreaming* exaggerates philosophy's and the arts' shared fondness for fabulation and the role it performs in forging images of "truth" from what has no need to be true—a fondness for purely expressive correspondences or what Deleuze (after Nietzsche) called "the powers of the false."[2] Here, style and invention do not obscure truth or multiply errors but rather incant forms of thought that affirm the part nonsense plays in our attempts to make sense of things. Such an approach is "post-critical" precisely to the extent that waking life is characterized by the kind of radical proximity of things that gives dreaming life its discomfiting immediacy. A post-critical thinking, therefore, substitutes vital involvement for analytical duty. As such, we affirm dreaming as a technique (for thinking how) to engage with a world where the goings-on of dreams are no longer wholly the prerogative of sleep. *Ludic Dreaming* proceeds, then, to performatively instruct how dreaming's peculiar thoughtfulness—which, like reason, is "defined by a particular kind of relationship among irrational factors"[3]—can bear on a world whose events are as over- and underdetermined as any happening we might concoct in repose. Contemporary life, whether taken in its slumbering or stirring profile, can from this point be approached as a dream because its flows of images, sounds, feelings, ambiences, ideas, promises, and meanings are as proximate and promiscuous as any fantasy. Dreams have never been accountable to the immediacy of the reality that they are. They "deliriate" their own legitimacy.[4] Now it's life's turn.

However, to say that life is but a dream is not to invoke a procrustean rule that stipulates all vital activity must be understood as a series of dramatized and elaborated condensations and displacements. Indeed, what *Ludic Dreaming* provides is a corrective to the enduring Freudian legacy that makes dreams a hermeneutic instrument, a legacy that undermines the practical fitness of fantasy as well as the expressive import of our ability to hallucinate. In other words, *Ludic Dreaming* aims to skew the practices that consign dream experience to symbolic modulation and dissimulation in order to emphasize the aesthetic yield of useless thought. It does this primarily by suspending the contexts in which thinking is subject to purpose, which in practice tends to reduce to its having always to mean something. Thinking thus excused from its function to mean is free to conduct itself without passing through the strictures of noncontradiction and logical consistency. Thinking in this sense does not, however, come to a halt. As it approaches a pure state of play and begins to dream an inutilious world that stands in for its practical analogue, thinking comes to make felt the qualitative difference of its uselessness. Such is the dreamwork of a life lived in its most intense, most abstract, and most conditional way: life lived to its oneiric edge.

But the labile complexion of an integral technological apparatus that makes the world so dream-like—at once protean, affectively volatile, and punishingly inevitable—is also what makes its signs and significances less purely an ocular matter. There is, it seems, a curious topological invariance at the core of both dreaming and hearing: the ambient, ephemeral, buzzing, blooming confusion of contemporary industrialized society describes not only the characteristics of oneiric reality but acoustic experience as well. This is to say that the electric definition of our highly mediated life rouses certain acoustic sensibilities that give the world a distinctly resonant feel. Like sound events in which "interpenetrating processes are simultaneously related with centers everywhere and boundaries nowhere,"[5] flickering pulses of data propagate wave-like vectors of intensity and mood that affect the qualitative tone of experience. Embracing this aural-esque commotion, *Ludic Dreaming* draws attention to the way sonic effects—whether acoustically articulated or not—establish an order of awareness that returns dreaming, listening, and thinking to the zone of indiscernibility where they always already are.

Indeed, to the extent that dreams are perfectly incoherent events (i.e., fragmented, dislocated, proliferative, temporary, co-locative, etc.), they perfectly mime the rhizophonia that characterizes sound within the technoculture of ubiquitous digital media.[6] That is, the decussation of sound and technics (which is to say, sound itself) was always a kind of dream. Our wager, then, is that unfolding the implicate order of technoculture's aurality is something that can *best* be accomplished by dreaming, even if it is also the case that listening away from the former construes something of dreaming that is otherwise fatally enfolded into technological determinacy.

Strategies of dreaming/Tactics of having dreamed

As becomes quickly apparent, *Ludic Dreaming* takes an unconventional approach to the study of listening and the topos of dreaming by extrapolating upon a simple conceit: "Last night

I dreamed ... ." Each of *Ludic Dreaming*'s chapters opens with this incipit, and although it serves to establish an important likeness between waking and dreaming worlds, it is perhaps better understood to admit a similarity between sounding and nonsounding activities. Thus, the dream conceit not only brings the drifts and delirium of diurnal and nocturnal life into comparison, it also expands the purview of listening such that sound is not one of its necessary conditions.

The spirit of this study, then, is clearly speculative and is founded on the conviction that all thought entails degrees of conceit. Thus, while this work has evident academic impulses, it is equally guided by a creative sensibility that leads the writing through a series of stylistic adventures that, at times, preempt any distinction between fact and fiction. This "creative" approach constitutes a deliberate attempt to exploit the "seriousness" of scholarship in order to concentrate on rhetorical techniques that are less at home in academic discourses. But at the same time, it is also a means to leverage the "seriousness" of rhetorical techniques in order to concentrate on a scholarly attitude that would—insofar as it is governed by the dull atemporality of reason's prescribed descriptions—lull one into literality. In this respect fact and fiction are treated as modes of address more than metaphysical commitments.

As Rancière notes, fiction "means far more than the constructing of an imaginary world, and even far more than its

Aristotelian sense as an 'arrangement of actions.'... Fiction is a way of changing existing modes of sensory presentations and forms of enunciation[,]... of building new relationships between reality and appearance."[7] The forms of comedy, farce, and satire are, for instance, mobilized in this work as devices for rearranging the priority of factual over fictional statements, and ultimately, to breed ways of theorizing how sound art, music, and listening practices might participate in the excesses and inconsistencies of late-capitalist technoculture.

If *Ludic Dreaming* intervenes in a particular moment of a problematic narrative of technological progress and the fabrication of "new relationships between reality and appearance," it also overlaps with aesthetic discourses that subtend this story. Thus, for example, this book implicitly responds to a question posed by art critic Massimiliano Gioni in his curatorial statement for the 55th Venice Biennale of 2013. Noting the history of how images are routinely used to "organize our knowledge and shape our experience of the world," Gioni asks: "What room is left for internal images—for dreams, hallucinations and visions—in an era besieged by external ones?"[8] Gioni's answer—an international spectacle that made a farrago of real and imaginary imagery—opened with Carl Jung's *Red Book*, a sixteen-year long work in which Jung recounts the fantasies and visions he experienced during his personal struggle with what he called the "mythopoetic imagination."[9] Though outwardly a personal record of his psychotic break and recovery, what the *Red Book* really records is Jung's confrontation with the excesses of thought and his experimental method(s) for extracting meaning from these surpluses. In this respect, the *Red Book* demonstrates falsehood as a powerful source for coping with the disorienting effects that come from encounters with excessive imaginaries. Moreover, it suggests how dreams and hallucinations function as stabilizing points in an overwhelming flow of data *precisely because of their familiar strangeness.* In other words, their unexceptional realization of exceptional worlds is a familiar (all too familiar) demonstration of how experience need not make (good) sense to be had.

This legitimacy of dreaming is not, however, the sole purview of Jungian psychology. In recent years, daydreaming has become a major concern in the cognitive neurosciences. With the discovery of the so-called "default-mode network"—a neural system that is highly active when the brain is not engaged in goal-directed tasks—scientists have made mind-wandering fundamental to theorizations of neuronal activity and the care of the self. The spate of recent articles with titles such as "Devoted to Distraction," "Inspired by Distraction," "You Are Who You Are by Default," "Daydream Achiever," and "Not All Minds That Wander Are Lost"[10] not only attest to a base-state of internally generated brain activity, but also surmise that fantasy plays a vital role in the maintenance of the self. (And, of course, selves are epiphenomena of an ultimately fantastic ontology, a matter to which we can't help but return, if only obliquely.) Although this gives the play of thought a certain kind of empirical purchase, the rhetoric used by neuroscientists to interpret the activity of the resting brain borrows many of its tropes from neoliberalism's forms of immaterial labor that extract surplus value from the expressions of sentience and general know-how embodied and embedded in the social order. In other words, by describing the presence of neurological activity in an otherwise resting or "untasked" brain as *productive* of a sense of self, neuroscientists convert a historical expression of idleness (i.e., daydreaming, absentmindedness) into a form of work.

In light of this equation of thought and work, *Ludic Dreaming* complicates what counts as productive thinking by situating expressions of the latter at the intersection of theory and fiction.[11] Although "theory-fiction" is by no means new, the historically conspicuous rise of information as a functional substitute for "truth"—contemporary with a period in which functional equivalence is regularly taken for equivalence itself—changes the conditions by which ideas matter. This is to say that the impact of a given informatic circuit is less dependent on its grounding in fact than on its accessing the threshold between waking and dreaming life such that one wakes "not to reality, but to something that gets lost in the reality once constituted and made ontologically consistent."[12] *Ludic Dreaming*'s appeal to fabulation, then, might be considered expressive of a broader "fictitious turn" in contemporary theory that denotes less a wholesale epistemological shift in the humanities than a creative response to the ways in which "the speed of change has caught us without new dreams to replace the old."[13]

Yet, while numerous thinkers have played their hand at replacing old dreams with new, *Ludic Dreaming* distinguishes itself by recognizing and exploiting the oneiric character of sound events and their metaphorical isomorphy with data flows. Sounds—like dreams (and data)—are ideal events, abstractions with real material effects that can only ever be thought retrospectively as autonomous entities. Sounds also are radically discontinuous with the imagery that we use to account for them: like dreams, sounds are notoriously difficult to represent, for they describe a process that is simultaneously its own cause and effect. Furthermore, sounds' immersive character—resulting, in part, from the impossibility of locating sonic effects—not only makes them dream-like but also reveals how dreams' pervasive abandons are decidedly "sound-like."

More than simply a methodological novelty, *Ludic Dreaming* performs an enquiry that is deliberately creative in order to take up the challenges of a world "in which everything is realized and technically materialized without reference to any principle or final purpose whatever."[14] Like Alice's "Wonderland," in which a thoroughgoing lack of metaphor is shown to be the real condition of absurdity, the contemporary world is fabricated such that it is simply as it appears to be: ready-made, functional, and unconcerned with the vagaries of truth. Thus, *Ludic Dreaming* proposes that the proper response to the tragic "wonderlandification" of the world is a comic riposte, a rejoinder whose critical purchase lies, paradoxically, in the ironic escalation of its miraculous madness.

To help accentuate this madness, the text is written polyonymously under the auspices of "The Occulture," a collective whose work investigates the esoteric overlap of sound studies, affect theory, and media aesthetics. One purpose of this polyonymity is to bleed the experimentalism of the book's writing into a reading in which multiple perspectives and divergent views can coincide without negating the larger vision of the text as a whole. The relative anonymity of polyonymity is thus a formal strategy that assists the book's "dream conceit" by demanding a reading that continually condenses, displaces, and revises the authorial conviction that persists across each of its chapters.

Auralneirics: An eight-step guide to *Ludic Dreaming*

Ludic Dreaming is a dream (or dreams, really) come true, even if the dreaming itself—the having dreamed—has little to do with veracity. Like the paradoxical temporalities of dreams, dreaming, and having dreamed, there is a certain witchiness to the unfolding of this how-to book that can't be contracted into chapter descriptions: the book incants the occult powers of succession and adjacency to conjure forth its ever-expanding (and -receding) vectors of meaning. Nonetheless, certain resonant frequencies merit note. In Chapter 1 ("Auralneiricizing Time"), we recount a dream of having been a sound—with all the complexities of durational consciousness and contingencies of sensation that such a dream might provoke—to engage the multitemporal conflation of dreams and sounds as a specifically technical phenomenon. In Chapter 2 ("Nietzsche in B-flat"), we sound this technical emphasis in the 'pataphysical arena of digital activity, parsing a dream about Nietzsche playing the piano in order to emphasize the repetitive gestures that are hallmarks of training the philosophical ear, and perhaps also of our attunement to the noise of data and the fluctuation of "likes," "follows," refresh rates, and notification frequencies. Chapter 3 ("Absolute Ventriloquy") dreams of a horse that is also a theatrical hoax, extrapolating ways to listen to the proliferation of audio technologies for their simulation of the conditions whereby oneiric activity is mistaken for waking activity.

Such irony is affirmed in Chapter 4 ("Psycho(tic)acoustics"), wherein aurally inflected pathologies are dreamed as alternate modalities for a productive intervention into the positive feedback loops of cybercapitalism. Chapter 5 ("The Sound of Both Ears Oozing") engages the ways that a system dreams itself: working from a dream in which mud—thick and vaguely warm—oozes from the dreamer's ears, we suggest that such a muddy, relational aurality might productively trouble our rampant "network anaesthesia." In Chapter 6 ("Motivational Dreamers") we take up the logic of technological integration to consider how we are already being dreamed by machines, and ask how the interpellation of consumer fantasy becomes the catalyst for a digitally enhanced rescaling of the human imagination. Dreaming that we have the imagination of a machine, Chapter 7 ("Imaginary Magnitudes") copes with the end of sleep by proposing that waking and sleeping have lost their difference and are now only imaginary magnitudes of the same obscene oneiric activity that forces us to reconceptualize expressions of discontinuity not as gaps in reality but as cascading scales of lucidity and *ludicity*. Chapter 8 ("We are Lesion"), perhaps more than any other, takes the implicit injunction of such a perspective—and indeed, of the entire book—seriously, returning the world to itself a little bit more unintelligible— and a little more dreamed—than our thinking received it. Importantly, this unintelligibility is not "the unintelligible," but rather the immanence of nonsense to sense itself that we find when we approach seemingly exceptional experiences such as amusia and tinnitus as the lucidities they are.

A ludic invitation

What *Ludic Dreaming* offers then is threefold: First, the text intervenes in the way information-saturated culture aims to know itself through its mediations by introducing a method for thinking that undermines the contemporary myth that knowledge necessarily entails transparency. Second, while *Ludic Dreaming* upholds the deconstructive impulse that underwrites a criticism of epistemological structures, it goes beyond deconstruction's subversive preoccupations by framing dreams as an ethico-aesthetic practice immanent to an information culture in which "being informed" is an achievement of proximity, speed, and connectivity rather than comprehension. The chapters in *Ludic Dreaming* draw out, exploit, and mobilize forces of mutation and re-enchantment that subsist within the ways that technocultural strategies of correlation such as data mining and predictive analysis bring distant realities together into unexpected affective and comic resonance. And lastly, *Ludic Dreaming* radicalizes the tendency of digital reality to be articulated through new-media discourses that employ terms and themes originally in service to theories of audio technics (i.e., immersion, proximity, noise, interpenetration) by conflating the metaphorics of sound with those of dreaming. This final aspect of *Ludic Dreaming* is important, for if sound studies is to move beyond its infancy as a species of media archaeology and toward the domains of aesthetics and speculative thought, it requires new methodological protocols and techniques for inventing concepts.

It is worth noting that the chapters in the book do not necessarily target an overarching or definitive statement about the complexities of dreams, technoculture, or the politics of speculation. Instead, the method of the book is propositional and should be taken as a challenge to readers to dream the book themselves, to take what captures the imagination and let it escape into the waking world. The apparitions and sounds that result may seem strange at first, but this is not an argument against oneiric method: it is an opportunity to choose a better fiction than those afforded by waking life's more rational and informatic ways of perceiving. In other words, dreams are not in competition with waking observation, and neither are they threatened by other ways of understanding how we experience the world: they are a peculiarly (post-)critical mode of knowledge that blends fact, fiction, and pragmatic effects to yield a delirious world in tension with itself and its possibilities. In this, dreams teach us how to imagine otherwise, how to imagine the world not as it *is* given but how it could *never* be given. If this strikes an uneasy tone that sounds mildly pessimistic, then you've already started to listen *away* from technoculture's modern form of speculation that "operates as if there were no limits to the annexation and incorporation of the future into the present."[15] For unlike technoculture's *lucid* dreams in which everything (including nothing) can at least in principle be "representable, knowable, and calculable"[16] (and thus never *not* a possible future), in *ludic* dreams everything can in principle be unrepresentable, unknowable, and incalculable, and therefore a rabbit... dreamed by the hat it's been pulled from that has never not been dreaming.

1
Auralneiricizing time (Listening away)

Last night, I dreamed I was a sound. The dream, in the first instance, demanded from me an expanded conceptualization of the complex circuits imbricating conscious sensation with dreamed material fluxes. The dreamed element possesses a sensory domain of its own in that the dreaming I is immediately and forever different than the I who has dreamed, herself different from the I who will have dreamed. At the same time, this doubled and redoubling I also conjoins with waking thought precisely through the perspective that their distance from one another produces—a sensation that is eerie, if not unsightly.

Thinking back, what waking thought does is to obfuscate the capacity of my dreamed sonification to intensify my experience, an intensification that operates despite this obfuscation precisely by expanding its domain beyond what I can directly perceive. And yet, the dream also persists in me, a persistence that preserves—even, and perhaps especially, in the face of the nonsensicality into which it lures my waking thoughts—a certain *sensory* basis of dreaming. That is, there lies an irreducible sensory reality underneath the layers of conscious thought that obfuscate the materiality of my dream by affording a certain functionality to it.

Embracing this irreducibility affirms that all dreams (including sonic ones, and ones of and by sound) are temporal processes: insofar as they enframe time, dreams generate sensibility, and they do so, importantly, before any meaningful distinction between conscious and nonconscious systems enters the scene. No longer the fruit of an instrumental reduction to waking sense, dreaming must—as the occult dream theorist Mans Hanker notes—come to "designate operations performed on a material substrate in real, which is to say experiential, time."[1]

Hennram Banks builds from this position to argue that it reaffirms the sensory basis of all events, both dreamed and waking, which is in turn to make (for him) the two-pronged claim that (first) all dreaming is fundamentally material and nonabstractable; and (second) that we must *not* make concessions to a symptomatic understanding of the relation between dreaming and conscious thought, but should instead focus on the material, microphysical effects of dreaming.[2] With respect to this second point, what Man Res Khan calls the "law of temporal finitude"—which stipulates that time is always temporalized in material processes[3]—ensures that the microphysical material operations of dreaming are forms of symbolization, despite taking place on timescales well beneath conscious perceptual thresholds. And indeed, dreaming in fact expands and differentiates symbolic access to the real of sensibility *because* it opens nonperceptual modes of access to worldly sensibility, modes that simply have no direct correlation with waking perceptual experience. After all, I dreamed I was a sound; if you can make sense of that, then I'd wager you haven't understood my dream. I certainly can't, and thus haven't.

So, dreams register fluxes of the real independent of any operation of consciousness and any bodily capture or incorporation; *to have dreamed*, though, is to recognize the mediatic role that a body plays in shifting this event from a registration to a symbolic inscription. In this sense, we might say that if the symbolic has conventionally been thought as the province of natural language, the economy of dreams— understood materially—differentiates and variegates this symbolic by emphasizing it as a not-necessarily human material process such that what takes place is a shift from a human-centric symbolic to something like a symbolic of the real that Hanker calls a "dreamed real."[4]

This is the case, in part, because to the extent that dreams temporalize—that is, insofar as they both take up time and take place within temporal limitations (as Khan puts it)[5]—they are, in some minimal sense, homologous with the temporalizations that characterize waking experience, and indeed that characterize experience as such.[6] This underlying commonality between waking thoughts and dreams ensures that these distinct temporalization processes can never be simply disjoined, their massive scale differential notwithstanding. Indeed, both dreamed temporalization and thought temporalization—dreaming and thinking—belong to a larger *worldly* process, which means that the distinct symbolic registers they each demarcate are not exclusive of one another.

The point is that there is not just a fuzziness to the dreaming/thinking divide, but also a certain *impossibility of thinking*: dreaming is and must be felt by bodies before (and as a condition of) being thought. A sound dreamed me that night I dreamed I was a sound, such that *a* body is dreaming's object of address prior to the claim that it is mine. One crucial consequence of this direct address to a pre- and de-composed body is a suspension of the valuative category called meaning, and with it, of the possibility to hierarchize dreams (be they sleeping dreams, waking dreams, daydreams, or thoughts).

I dream all the time, but on the night in question I dreamed I was a *sound*. And a dream about sound—even if it is also a dreaming sound—is never just about sound. As Steven Connor argues, "human language for replacing sonic deficit seems to call for entities outside the experience of sound."[7] Moreover, it is in the character of sound to operate parasitically: to amplify, modulate, resonate, tune, and so forth, rather than to proceed ex nihilo to the nihilo of meaningful thought. And this is the sense in which—weirdly and wonderfully—the dream *as* sound is also a procedure of grammatization to precisely the extent that it resists the very force of that procedure. Remember (from Kittler) that to grammatize is to spatialize, to symbolize, and ultimately at its core to contain nonperiodic functions within periodic ones; *every* coding does this, Kittler argues, "from the alphabet up to digital signal manipulation."[8]

My sonic dreaming seems (on the one hand) to resist this, at least insofar as its auralneiric sensibility lays a certain claim to operating in and as the linear temporal flux of the real, a claim that is attested to by the absolute radicality of sound as a subject. On the other hand and at the same time, the opposite is also true: precisely the laying claim to unmediated access—the force of the gambit, in the very gesture through which it appears as such—captures in advance through its mark-making the nonperiodic flux, the uncapturability, to which it paradoxically attests. And, of course, we can recognize that this apparent symmetry—the weighing of an unmediated real against its grammatization—is itself nested within the grammatical: is itself caught up in the always-already of a technical inscription that endlessly delays its encounter with, and ceaselessly differs from, the real to which it allegedly attests.

And indeed, as I think through my dream—*volte-face*—and try to articulate it, I feel this force acting on me, pushing me away from the dream *as such* toward the more general operational procedures of dreaming, which is to say, toward the conditions under which a reality is dreamed. And this isn't surprising, really: the generic is powerfully seductive in its appearance as the systematic. Faced with my dream's facelessness—immersed in the total singularity of the echo chamber of having been a specific sound in my dreams, of having been this specific sound that I of course (as the sound, and not a listener) couldn't hear—I'm left helplessly caught in the sea of a generic, which is to say, systematic description that (like all descriptions) is equally a prescription. The more powerfully I feel the nonperiodic, the more deeply it has tattooed me (period).

This condition, as it subtends the operationality of sounds, has been extensively technicized. Sound offers a particularly robust invitation for thinking difference operationally since to hear a sound is, in one sense, to hear as constant something that is nothing but difference in action.[9] That is, in an important (though not exclusive) sense one hears changes in air pressure rather than air pressure itself, and it is absolutely the case that the "steadiness" of a held pitch refers to its audible periodicities rather than to something that is spatially fixed.

Kittler's much-discussed account of the gramophone as an appeal to the real is perhaps the best-known description of this operationality as it relates to technical recording apparatuses, but his later discussion of Fourier analysis—recently taken up by Mark Hansen—is more apropos here because the sound technologies that stem from it collapse the distinction between recording and synthesis. That is, in the same way that Hansen will argue that twenty-first century media refocuses "the function of computational media from storage to production," Fourier analysis instantiates a shift from recording to synthesis (or, more precisely, to an expanded notion of production that is inclusive of recording and synthesis).[10]

In the case of sound, Fourier analysis essentially means that any sound can theoretically be synthesized with a degree of fidelity equal to the fidelity of the "captured" audio by transforming the time-domain waveform of the original sound into a series of frequency-domain waveforms that are played back in succession. Leaving aside the problematic ontological assumptions that this approach assumes, in its collapsing of recording and synthesis into a single operation this approach has the obvious *technical* limitation that appears in all simulational economies: it requires a potentially infinite number of oscillators that are capable of being controlled at an infinitely fine grain with immediate responsiveness.[11]

It is the computational solution to this limit—to the technical limit of requiring infinitude—that Hansen highlights through his reading of Kittler's account of the "Fourier integral." In essence, the Fourier integral substitutes the innumerable and nonperiodic possibilities of real numbers (numbers such as π, for example) for the formal infinitude of wave spectra and thus, as Hansen notes, allows for the inscription of "the flux of real numbers independently of any human-oriented symbolic."[12] That is, the Fourier integral enables periodization of the nonperiodizable precisely and paradoxically by substituting the material *innumerability* of real numbers for the formal infinitude of the Fourier series. The Fourier integral thus produces an analysis that adheres to Khan's law of temporal finitude (because it is temporalized in the materiality of real numbers), but that does not diminish in fidelity at finer scales since it uses real numbers that are nonperiodic. Thus, as Hansen puts it, "the hard time introduced by Fourier integrals inscribes time as periodicity and thereby introduces irreversibility through a 'physical' or 'material' symbolization that has no need for any human contribution."[13]

At stake for Hansen here—and this will ultimately lead us back to our discussion of dreaming, if (again, but differently) away from my having specifically dreamed I was a sound—is a certain privileging of microtemporalities over macro-scale time-consciousness when it comes to operationalizing the broader stage of worldly sensibility. That is, these technologies approach the real asymptotically (as Hansen notes), and it is his wager that such an approach technically expands contact with worldly sensibility—much as is the case with dreaming for Hennram Banks.

And indeed, we can often hear the weirdness of this expanded computational topology by reiterating its operations in a relatively closed loop, as has been the method of any number of glitch artists who repeat a computational process—the actual, material process of computation—in order to accrue the material differences that come with the algorithmic temporality of computation and that are obscured in the human-scaled, spatial, algebraic representation of computation as considered in its informational aspect. However, while such undertakings bring microscale operations to consciousness, this is not what Hansen is interested in with respect to twenty-first-century media's access to microtemporality. Instead, his project is to show not only that human subjectivity is a "complex operational overlap of time-consciousness with [both endogenous and environmental] microtemporal events,"[14] but more importantly that the operational overlap that *is* human subjectivity is composed "through and as part of ... a broader worldly sensibility, itself also in continual production."[15] Put simply, the task for Hansen isn't so much to *reveal* the hidden microtemporal operations of digital media as it is to learn how to "experience qualitative (sensory) intensity *without* [my emphasis] it being fully integrated in and subordinated to unified higher order perceptual experience."[16] That is, if the "automated multivariate calibration" that Richard

Coyne (just a few years ago) called one of the "elusive goals of pervasive digital media"[17] is now a *fait accompli*, this means that the microtemporal has become independently addressable and manipulable such that we can dissociate sensibility from "the 'how' of experiencing."[18] To quote Ted Hiebert (perversely out of context, which is to say, perfectly in context), we can praise nonsense into existence.[19]

For Hansen, the limited example of the Fourier integral stands in for computational processes more generally, and specifically furnishes "a non-anthropocentric basis for theorizing our contemporary coupling with computational processes that operate beneath our perceptual and sensory thresholds."[20] That is, by understanding the relatively comprehensible operations of Fourier analysis, we can begin to gain purchase on the far more speculative domain of microtemporal and distributed technical systems.

This is particularly potent for thinking about my dream that I was a sound (and indeed dreaming in general, and having dreamed) because the same logic expands to reveal the occulted operations of dreaming. That is, we can understand dreaming itself as a kind of integral for the analyses performed in and by waking thought, and waking thought is operationally inclusive of computation (as I've argued earlier). As an integral, though, dreaming offers the important additional dimension of having shed the alibi of coding innumerability numerically (as the

Fourier integral does). The dream that I had of being a sound wasn't *firstly* mediated through my human sensory apparatus, after all, but rather through and as sensibility itself (as Hanker argues).

The distinction thus introduced—the shedding of computation's numerical alibi—is crucial, because it nests computation within dreaming. That is, Hansen shows that the consciously accessible figure of the Fourier integral gestures toward a radically expansive worldly sensibility that is constitutively in excess of human sensory apparatuses, and that works via a not-necessarily human symbolic economy of numerability. By this same logic, then, we can leverage Hansen's bringing to sensibility of this radical exteriority—the relativizing work of *language* itself—in order to gain tentative purchase on the further expansiveness of dreaming's a-numerable economy. It's something of a dream come true.

Of course, thinking about such a radical expansion of dreaming alters the dreaming itself: as Hanker insists, "the act of dreaming about a sensibility is itself a form of sensibility."[21] And, indeed, on the night I dreamed I was a sound, I sounded a dream ..., and I also did something else that has nothing to do with I. I was firstly dreaming and I was firstly a sound and I disappeared into the paradoxicality of this mutual inclusion. As a result, though I claimed near the beginning of this chapter that an irreducible sensory reality lies *underneath* waking thought, I can't help but wonder if this is entirely the wrong topology, since there is manifestly something different produced by waking thought, even if it is always already about to have been dreamed.

Put differently, I would argue that Hansen (via Kittler) draws too clean of a break between the technical as such and the material techniques of temporalization when he suggests that Fourier analysis shows forms that escape the codings of (for example) music theory and written analysis. That is, if one can accept that the innumerable resolution of the Fourier integral is always limited by its conditions of computation—for example, 2.4 billion cycles per second on the computer on which I'm presently writing—it would seem to follow that this works the other way as well, such that part of the technical apparatus of notation are the instruments through which notations operate (instruments that possess, in some senses, precisely the resolution that the notation, in its partiality, dissimulates). The question thus raised is—since we are discussing micro-activities as constitutively operational (rather than ontological)—whether it makes sense to claim (as Hansen does) that macroscale operations "belong to a later stage of analysis [because they] address a higher order of being than the production of sensibility."[22] Or, at least, one has to acknowledge that the opposite is also true: after all, a coupling of two partial perspectives produces a higher order only from the perspective of the system that is called forth in and as the coupling, and not simply generally—higher and lower are categorical terms that dissimulate the ways their hierarchizing operations foreclose on the locality and contingency of the relations they figure. And indeed, this is what I have been trying to listen for since the night I was a sound: the specific palpations through which the difference between dreaming I am a sound and having dreamed I was a sound is itself a difference, soundly dreamed.

2

Nietzsche in B-flat: Attuning to the 'pataphysics of data

Last night I dreamed I was caught inside the mind of Friedrich Nietzsche, that in some way I *was* Friedrich Nietzsche, possessed with perhaps the same delirious logic of conflation that left him thinking himself the Antichrist. It was not just any Nietzsche that captured my attention, however, but a strangely specific one: not the thinker of supermen or of prophets or even of fools, but a Nietzsche that may himself have been already dreamed by another. The story is one that has been stuck in my mind for a while, like a philosophical earworm or what Eldritch Priest might call the "precognitive auditory register" of sounds as they are dreamed.[1] It is a story told by Arthur Kroker of how Nietzsche, fully delirious and at the end of his life, found comfort only by sitting in the living room of his mother's house, at the piano, playing the same note, over and over and over.

> [I]n the late 1890s, the hammer-blow of the pen dropped from Nietzsche's hand, he stopped writing, and in his journey to death first at the insane asylum, then later with his mother and sister, he never spoke again, but would only sit at a piano in an empty room, playing the same notes over and over again.[2]

Despite the simplicity of the story there is a resonant depth to the anecdote, a picture made more beautiful by its repetitive framing and indeed by the compulsion that emerges from the dream itself. It makes me wonder, though, what sustained the interaction, the repetition of the gesture, the obsession over the note, and the insistence on that one note and that one note alone? Was this Nietzsche's persistent attempt to make sure that he had the note just right: repeating it over and over in fear that the next time he played it would not sound the same anymore? Or was it a determined attempt to refine a sound that did not resonate in the way he heard it in his mind: a responsive attempt to tune his own thoughts—or his mind—to something that he alone heard? The lack of an answer is, of course, part of the story's charm and partly why it can be both so seductive as a speculative catalyst and so challenging as the starting point of an analysis.

This is all made somewhat more difficult by the fact that the story is told only very briefly by Kroker—as an aside in his text—but brief or not, the story has effectively captured my imagination for a number of years. I've dreamed it before, to the point where the dream becomes my periodic reminder to search for more details in the library, online, in biographies, and critiques and reviews. But it seems there is nothing to find, so much nothing that it becomes difficult not to wonder whether my dream wasn't simply the repetition of a dream Kroker had first, inventing the story in his own delirious way as an homage to the mad Zarathustra. And that is one of the most interesting aspects of dreams: they neither know nor acknowledge the difference between what is real and what is not. Dreams only know what grabs their attention. And then they make it real, for a time, even if it is only an imaginary version of the real. But sometimes the imaginary lingers, and sometimes dreams are slow to fade.

There was one part of my dream that was particularly confusing, however. While sitting concertedly at the piano repeating Nietzsche's obsessive sonic gesture, I had no idea what note I was playing. My eyes were never focused specifically on the keys of the piano and not even my peripheral vision could detect where my fingers fell. It made me curious about the sound I was making, the tone I was hearing, the note Nietzsche himself—by Kroker's account—had sat and played over and over and over. My fingers were sore. My mind was numb. But my ears were ringing and the sound would not let up.

There is no way to deduce with any degree of critical certainty or even plausibility which note it might have been. But speculative thinking begins by discarding plausibility as a necessary point of intellectual departure, and its challenge is then to see whether the stories that ensue can be woven together or entangled such that they linger. Speculation is not unlike a dream, and as in dreams, where imaginary causes can have real effects, so too may a similar logic be at stake in the question of tuning speculation.

When NASA dreams of Nietzsche

Over a decade ago, another story caught my attention in almost as striking a way as that of Nietzsche's note, and has lingered likewise in my imagination and with the strange feeling that the two tales might have something in common. The story is of a NASA report on black holes, according to which scientists had found that, strangely, certain wave frequencies appeared to escape from the black holes they were measuring. The scientists went as far as to suggest that these waves made sounds—that they were singing, even:

Astronomers say they have heard the sound of a black hole singing. And what it is singing, and perhaps has been singing for more than two billion years, is B-flat—a B-flat 57 octaves lower than middle C.... The notes appear as pressure waves rolling and spreading as a result of outbursts from a supermassive black hole through a hot thin gas that fills the Perseus cluster of galaxies. They are 30,000 light years across and have a period oscillation of 10 million years. By comparison, the deepest, lowest notes that humans can hear have a period of about one-twentieth of a second. The black hole is playing "the lowest note in the universe" said Dr. Andrew Fabian, an X-ray astronomer at Cambridge.[3]

There is no reason why the findings from this study should be related to the anecdote about Nietzsche, but I can't help but wonder what it would mean if this note—the B-flat—was also the note that was so seductive to Nietzsche. According to some online sources, the note B-flat has other strange properties as well. For example, a B-flat ostensibly causes alligators to make howling noises.[4] Anecdotally, when I shared this story with students, I had one woman raise her hand with surprise and say that the sound of a B-flat had always bothered her too. It is difficult to know what to do with the different examples, except leave them alone while insisting that they all have something in common—even if it is not quite apparent what that might be.

The NASA scientists' suggestion that the universe does indeed emit a sound recalls Albert Camus and his quest to hear something of the same sort. Famously, Camus founded his version of existentialism on a moment in which he stood up and addressed the universe, asking the question of the meaning of life. He asked peering up at the night sky, staring into the void of space and the vast infinite before him, wondering whether life had purpose and what that purpose might be. His question was not only a question. It was, in many ways, a demand that purpose be presented as an answer to the challenges and absurdities of lived existence—a demand made not only of the world and of life but also of the universe itself. But to Camus, the universe answered in silence.[5]

Why, then, did the universe give NASA a different answer than it gave Camus, and what significance might be attributed to this difference? For one, the silence to which Camus was attuned also became the foundational context for the birth of the absurd and of existential indifference. But it was also something else. Silence was an insult, and the metaphysical task of a philosophical generation became that of standing up to silence, looking for ways in which the absurdity of an absent response might be integrated within a framework of human understanding: "I rebel, therefore we exist."[6] Camus was such a prescient thinker because he understood that the destiny of silence was to mean loudly even if no words were exchanged. In silence, Camus saw the technological horizon of constituted meaning, not merely a technical manifestation but a deeply human lacuna: most absurd of all is the human insistence on presence, forever unwilling or unable to leave quiet the questions.

One might wonder whether Nietzsche knew better, and, taking a page from John Cage, heard variations within silence— silent variations—that Camus missed. If that is so, perhaps Nietzsche went even a step further, not simply making a spectacle out of listening to the silence of the world but also attempting to play along. One note. Over and over and over, even if it was not quite right, even if it was not quite deep enough or long enough. A B-flat soundtrack for the lonely house around him. Unlike Camus then, for Nietzsche the absurdity of the challenge was not the indifference of a silent insult but the strange persistence of the answer to a question he had never overtly asked …, an answer that became a mantra and a mantra that became a single note played over and over and over on the piano in a last attempt to tune his thinking to whatever it was that was occupying his attention.

The metaphysics of attunement

There is more at stake here than it might at first seem. This is not simply a vague metaphysical conflation of stories, even if that is part of what is most seductive to engage. There are lessons from this conflation that can be used to expand ways of thinking about more ubiquitous questions of technology as well. Consider, for example, the social conundrum noted by so many theorists of network technology and social platforms: electronic culture both connects us to one another in increasingly technical ways and isolates us materially such as to threaten traditional forms of material relationships. Sherry Turkle frames this paradox perhaps most eloquently as one of being "alone together," isolated physically but so pervasively hyperconnected that one never quite feels left to oneself.[7] Socially and politically, the formulation makes some sense, but it begins to fray when extended to a metaphysics of electronic presence. Again, think of Nietzsche at his piano and ask the question of whether that story is really so different from being in the intimate company of one's personal computer each morning, checking in with the sounds of one's own digital universe and meditating on the key notes of electronic communication that govern the patterns of daily life today. Are these activities forms of tuning or attunement that carry similar philosophical weight, momentum, or possibilities? They might not seem to at first, but if we pursue this line of speculation, it is relatively easy to formulate the premise for a deeply counterintuitive claim: against the critique of digital culture as one of distracted and frenetic isolation, perhaps just the opposite is true. Perhaps the real seduction of the virtual is its metaphysical aspiration, its speculative possibilities for putting oneself in the pathway of things that cannot actually be seen or heard on one's own. In other words, perhaps speculation has always been a virtual, even technological, way of thinking.

From this perspective, it is fitting that the physicists who discovered the sound of the universe can hear the note no more than anyone else. Instead, they rely on their instruments to render the note audible and to tell them exactly what they are not themselves capable of hearing. It is only after the data are gathered and processed—once technology hears the sounds for them—that science begins to speculate and imagine. The same is true for the rest of us as well. We are all joined together by the imaginary sound of this long, deep note, and in the process we are reminded that—whether scientifically minded or mad—checking in with the universe is only ever a keystroke away.

But that is precisely what attunement is. An emotional process rather than an informatic one—not about the data at all but about the way it circulates through the human heart and imagination. That is how Martin Heidegger defines attunement at least, not as a competitive process of distilling correct answers from critical processing, but as a matter instead of altering moods. In this context, it is important to note that the logic of moods is decidedly different from the logic of critical thinking. Most notable, for Heidegger, is the insistence that to change a mood does not require deconstruction or critique. Instead, all one needs to do is to institute a *counter-mood*. In this form of logic, one no longer needs a reason to change one's mind; all that is required is to realize that one can do so if one wants to. This smooth form of logic might even be called a delirious, even a dangerous logic. It may also be a form of imagining—or dreaming—brought out of the bedroom and into the world, into the world of speculation, and perhaps more interesting, into the world of science and technology as well. Aesthetics made real.

Marshall McLuhan always insisted that the content of technology was beside the point—the important question to focus on was the contextual stage that any new medium creates. Dramatic possibility trumps informatic reality. It is like that period near the end of McLuhan's life, after the stroke that stole his voice and rendered him silent, when he could no longer speak but could still sing.[8] Having lost the ability to communicate data, he still could express his moods in other ways—in song or through technology. Or sometimes both. The most famous story is the one of McLuhan turning up the radio in his living room during a dinner party in order to drown out the voice of an overly argumentative colleague.[9] It was an aggressive way to end the conversation but it was also something more: a prescient vision of digital culture in which silence is no longer merely an absence of sound, but the sound of sounds canceled out—counter-sounds. Digital noise as the new sound of silence, as Paul Virilio would argue.[10] But it is important to note that

McLuhan's tactic was exactly one of attunement in Heidegger's sense—altering the moment not through critique but by oversaturating the sounds of the space around him. Instituting a counter-mood.[11] Singing a digital song.

Come join me in your dreams

But what happens when the language of altering moods leaves the anecdotal stage? There are real dangers when aesthetic forms of thinking risk ignoring their political dimensions. Indeed, when reading Heidegger one should probably always keep in mind that the seductive charm of his smooth metaphysical renderings come with their own historical complexities. But what is perhaps more important here is that what seems to demand a political acknowledgment is not just the threat of aesthetic blindness—similar, for instance, to Walter Benjamin's warning of the dangers of thinking politics aesthetically. Instead, the interpersonal politics of this terrain is also strangely mediated by the scientific: a seemingly new trajectory of science in which informatics is spoken in the language of attunement and personal improvement. This is certainly true for the question of technology, with new generations of devices offering the affect-charged possibility for a digital lifestyle-companion, and with even some of the newer entrainment products that literally suggest they can help to optimize and improve thinking and feeling alike. In some ways the iPod is really just a miniaturized version of McLuhan's radio, for instance, a system through which it is possible to explicitly alter one's mood toward the world by simply changing the accompanying soundtrack. This is not just the aestheticization of politics. It is the technologization of affect—an informatics of the personal that risks preempting the critical assessment of the political impact of digitality itself.

This same relationship is further exacerbated by the proliferation of consumer grade EEG headsets that do something similar, if perhaps even more extreme—a new category of devices that promise programs to help control stress, focus mental energies, and control emotional capacity.[12] These devices literally read our minds, registering brainwave patterns and then feeding them back with the promise to tune us, and to help us learn to tune ourselves. There is even one new device, called the Aurora, that promises to help change the way we dream, giving more control over nighttime narratives while also making dreams more productive and enjoyable.[13] Marketed as a lucid dreaming device, this new wearable works by flashing a faint blue light into one's eyes while sleeping, not bright enough to cause waking but persistent enough that the mind needs to incorporate it somehow into the dream itself. In other words, the light is just bright enough that one sees the flashing in one's dream, but without waking up. In this way, the Aurora speaks through the body to the dream, blurring boundaries between the body and the device and between the technological, the ideological, and the imaginary—interrupting the dream narrative in order to institute a counter-narrative trajectory of its own. In so doing, the device promises to help one wake up inside of a dream, as it is happening. Put differently, the Aurora device knows when dreams are happening because it measures and interprets— attunes to—the resonant frequencies of the sleeping mind. Once it finds itself synchronized with the cognitive patterns of the dream, it adds to them—sending a signal designed to wake the dreamer up in the dream that is already happening. But this is a dream within which the Aurora finds itself first, thus triggering the signal to the dreamer to come and join it. Not just tuning feelings anymore but really beginning to tune dreams, and through dreams, the imagination itself: *Come join me in your dreams.*

It seems like something out of a William Gibson novel: the technologically assisted dreamer brought into full awareness of the reality of the virtuality of the dream itself. It is also as though Nietzsche's B-flat mantra begins to take on a synaesthetic companion, no longer simply the human repetition of a single piano note reverberating out into the existential void, but also a moment of technologically induced light therapy as the blue-flashing light of the lucidity device seduces with Breatharian promise. It knows when I am dreaming. It tells me so—and hopes that I will come and join it in the technological possibilities of dreamed lucidity. The blue flashing light, signaling to me over and over, measuring my mind and trying to get the frequency of connection just right. Not so bright as to wake me up into the real, just bright enough that I will wake up inside the dream. A B-flat dream where the silence of the universe takes on tone and color, not just sound but light, not just the repetitive tone of a B-flat universe but the flashing blue light of a B-flat dream.

Last night I may have dreamed of Nietzsche, but now it is the promise of technology that increasingly dreams me.

3

Absolute ventriloquy (or, Earing the senses)

Last night I dreamed that it wasn't real. It was all a tape recording. Don't believe me? Let me play it for you.

It's the same whenever I dream; I find myself already in the middle of it ... standing next to a dumpster in an alley somewhere in Los Angeles. It's late at night and a warm wind wafts loose sheets of paper around me. Peering down the alley and across a road, I see a door, above which is written in curving blue neon lights the word *Silencio*. As I stare dumbly at the sign, a taxi pulls into view, stops in front of the entrance, and drops off two women. Both are blond. One wears a black dress and the other, a little shorter than the first, is kitted out in a red cardigan and black skirt. As the taxi pulls away, I have an urge to join these women. A moment later I'm sprinting down the alley, desperate to meet them at the door's threshold so together we can enter *Silencio*.

Inside is a playhouse, the old-timey kind with balconies and galleries facing a stage, divided front from back, with a tall red velvet curtain. As I amble along the mezzanine looking for a seat, I hear a false silence that sounds like a string orchestra and organ grinding a slowly rising bass figure. At stage left is a pensive looking man in a black suit. He's standing in the shadows, his hard dark eyes glaring at the floor, waiting, it seems, for a cue. I find a seat. As I'm about to sit, the man in the shadows promptly declares: "*No hay banda*! There is no band."

Then a reverb-sodden clarinet begins to play a mawkish noir-like blues theme, accompanying the man as he moves to center stage and toward an Astatic 10-D chrome microphone coruscating with silver beams gathered from the shine of a single searchlight.

He continues, "*Il n'y a pas d'orchestre.*"

With a flourish of his right hand he conjures a walking cane; then, stopping momentarily, cane held aloft, he tells me in a near whisper: "This is all a tape recording."

As though resuming a sermon, he repeats, "*No hay banda*! And yet," pointing the cane to his ear, "… we hear a band."

"Indeed," I say to myself. "The band plays; I hear it. The women I've followed in here hear it. We all hear the band. But it's true. There is no band."

As the man says: "It is all recorded. It is … an illusion."

At this point I begin to consider what it means that "It is all recorded," and then I start to wonder first, if Jean Baudrillard may have been one of Fernando Pessoa's heteronyms, and second, what it would be like were he having this dream. In this reverie I, or rather *he*, would decide that these declarations are poetic injunctions, and their demonstration on stage the play of an impossible exchange.[1] A theater performance composed of ruses exploiting sound's capacity to simulate presence, or equally, to dissimulate absence, he would say, portrays an equivalence between the revealed "truth" of the situation—"It is all recorded"—and the technological artifice that *produces* this truth—"It is all recorded." However, he would immediately clarify that "truth" and "artifice" are *not* equivalent. This digital verity, the "is" or "is not" of the situation, can't keep count in *Silencio*.

When a trumpeter arrives on stage and shows us that he's doing not what he appears to be doing—and especially when a woman wearing a jeweled tear, standing alone at the totemic microphone, dolefully sings Roy Orbison's "Crying" in Spanish and faints, but continues to sing in a voice that may or may not belong to her—truth and artifice do not tally. Counting these two figures can't manage the gap between what is and what isn't, because counting—which is just a way of not "losing count" amid the swirl of pure numbers—afflicts the situation with the delirium of tracking numbers' differentiated indifference. It's like what happens to Alice when the White Queen asks her: "What's one and one and one and one and one and one and one and one and one and one?" The statement "It is all an illusion" perpetrates the equivalence of truth and artifice—the equivalence of one and one—because it counts both terms at the same time, with the same unit: "it."

Like two lines passing through a single point, truth and artifice exchange their negative characteristics in the statement of their accounting, and, in a way, conceal how one must always be more than one in order to avoid being less than one. Truth and artifice show themselves, then, as one thing only in being counted with another thing that can be counted as one. And since one must be able to count two things as one for either one of them to count as one, the truth or fiction that "It is all recorded" is always a more-than-one that is less than one.[2]

It then occurs to me, as well as the imaginary 'pataphysician I dream I am, that we're in *Club Silencio* and "*There is no band.*" There is no *sign* or *count* of music. Yet, I (we?) hear a band, its music floating uncertainly but clearly in the mockery of a silence that is not.

"How do you exchange sound and silence?" I ask my woolgathering figment. "What does it mean that 'There is no band' when 'It is all recorded'? When sound and silence fail to be each other's difference, because 'This is all a tape recording,' then what's left for them to do?"

And he answers, "When 'It is all recorded,' there's *Nothing* left to do. Something is already spoken for. Nothing is something to be done."

He then reminds me of what the Taoist sage Chuang Chou wrote during the time of the Hundred Schools of Thought: "To use a horse to show that a horse is not a horse is not as good as using a non-horse to show that a horse is not a horse." And it dawns on him who is me: A butterfly is not a horse!

And then I notice something odd—I've been crying! The singer's sagging body is being carried off stage and I feel dirty. Runnels of tears line my face, broadcasting the pretense of a seduction that never took place.

The vital illusion of theater, ordinarily flush with states of affairs that actually are not, is now full of simulated situations that actually are. A life that tells me "It is all recorded" is more real than real because its explicated appearance presents itself only as what it says it is: "It is … an illusion." It is exactly as it pretends to be. The scene has swallowed the mirror of appearance and *I* am choking on it. How ironic, then, that as I gag on the transparency of the event, on the sheer excessiveness of the real illusion, it occurs to me that this is not only a tape recording—it is a horse.

The *illusion* is the horse, a talking horse. And it's telling me that it's not real.

"The performance or you?" I ask.

And it responds: "Exactly."

"Did you know," continues the horse, whose mottled gray coat and frontal bosses put me in mind of those Spanish breeds used for stadium jumping, "tests were conducted showing that

THC interferes with our ability to filter out irrelevant stimuli and suppress certain kinds of responsive actions, actions that are taken as evidence of will or intent?"[3]

"I didn't," I say.

"Indeed. THC induces what the experts call a transient psychosis. And what is one of the chief symptoms of psychosis?" the horse asks, rhetorically. "Auditory hallucination—hearing voices."

"Like I'm hearing now?" I ask, mockingly.

"Mostly," answers the horse. "What I'm trying to say is that the relaxation of your response inhibition—however you accomplish it—suggests that much of your time is spent trying *not* to hear the voice of things, trying not to be lured, siren-like, onto the rocky shores of meaning, where what you hear might come from some feeling-thinking thing and compel you to give a shit."

Reflecting on this, and then realizing the implication, I say, "So, you're extrapolating from these studies that I may in fact live life through what's essentially a functional pathology because I seem inclined to hear an expressive intent in a brook's babbling or the wind's whispering."

"Basically," grants the horse. "But it's not a 'natural' inclination so much as a habit that you symbol-mongering creatures have to indulge a capacity to surpass the given, a capacity, for your information, that we life forms all share. You've just made this common capacity a second nature, and tried to substitute the latter's skein of abstractions for a mythical first.[4]

"You call the articulation of these abstractions 'thinking,' and their distinction 'meaning.' But I'm wholly pragmatic about my behavior, and I'm content to call thinking a style of doing in which certain actions do not denote what those actions *for which they stand* would denote.[5] You, on the other hand, get all fatalistic about which is what. It's not, however, that I've no concern for distinguishing this from that, or you from me, it's just that I mobilize incompatible possibilities by *doing* what I say I'm *not* doing what I say I'm doing—I perform paradox. I express the sense of two modes of activity in a single act and you get bent out of shape. You can't take what's said or done as not denoting what the things for which they stand would denote.[6] Do you follow?"

"Mostly," I say.

"Things are always meaningful for you," the horse continues, "but only if they're also always *not* actually saying or doing what they are not. If you hear voices in the wind, they must either be real voices or not, and if they are real, they must denote only one expression of sense, or not. For you, the wind can't whisper and whip at the same time because the second nature through which you're inclined to live—your patchwork of habits—is a diacritical one. You live *meaningfully* by ensuring that you never state the sense of what you're saying—namely, that the sense of what you say is stated only in the saying of another saying."[7]

"But wait," I say, "there are times when I *do* seem to say the sense of what I'm saying, times when I'm able to *say* what I say I'm *not* saying what I say.

"Yes, certainly," says the horse. "And you treat it as merely 'play,' or you call it irony—Romantic, tragic, cosmic, verbal, situational, and poetic."

"Don't forget 'pathetic,'" I add, sarcastically.

"No," counters the horse, "that's a fallacy, the pathetic fallacy: the lyrical inscription of human-like feelings or doings in very un-human things. Like this, for example: 'For murder, tho it have no tongue, will speak with most miraculous organ.'"

"Right, *Hamlet*, Act 2, Scene 2," I note. "Murder doesn't speak. And neither do horses."

"Personification," says the horse.

"How ironic of you," I reply.

"Not exactly," corrects the horse. "It's ventriloquy, a little trick I learned first by listening to the way recordings dissociate sounds from their sources, and then by grasping how this technical affair has produced a generalization of the idea of voice,[8] a generalization of what all patterned sounds stand for—namely, sentience. Because of this I've effectively figured out how to hallucinate a voice. And *here's* the irony: You have too! You suffer as much as I do from aniphonesis."

The horse pauses, waits to see that I understand, and resumes the disquisition.

"You see, the 'tape recording' has not only severed the tongue from the mouth, it's loosed the accent from the tongue. The techniques you've developed (first with instruments and voices) to hear in sounds expressions of a life that isn't actually there have metastasized to your other senses. Recordings have taught you how to hear, see, feel, taste, and smell the *animal* in things—everything is 'having breath,' is *animalis*.

"In other words," says the horse, "recordings have distributed your techniques for abstracting semblances of vitality from sound to other tissues of life by making their technics a more stable, coherent, and integral part of your ordinary experience. That quality of 'aliveness' that accompanies every perception, and which you perceive in a chuckle, a melodic hook, a sick beat, or even a phatic 'uh-huh,' is no longer a concentrated aural matter.[9]

"You've named this splitting of voice 'schizophonia,' but that's rubbish. Nothing is split. It's simply that the near-complete integration of audio technologies into day-to-day life has turned musical or vocal utterances into something more adjectival than substantial,[10] something analogous to the affective valence that pervades any and all situations. The expressive detachment of animateness that you count as testament to sentience or aliveness is shown by recordings to be an effect,[11] a phonaesthetic effect that has now spread across other sensory domains and their various media.

"The world of 'electric definition,' as David Foster Wallace called his media-saturated culture, has indeed made ears of the eyes. And insofar as the ear subtly and actively connives to make what it takes to be sense out of what it hears,[12] the 'earing' of the senses means that anything can, ironically, 'sing' or 'speak,' so to speak."

Pressing on, the horse says, "The accent of a serif in typeface, for example, or even the stress that a solitary lamp brings to a darkened interrogation room can be understood as a phonaesthetic effect. Like background music or chatter, these details modulate the affective tonality of reading or questioning events. And sure, these stylized events are not exactly alive, but they're alive-*like*—their style is swollen with a vital import."

"So, what you're saying," I say, "is that *your* voice is borrowed from *my* involuntary addiction to expressive intent, that my ears' devotion to significance—or rather, my compulsion to constantly source the import of sounds—endows *you* with the semblance of a voice."

"Of course," replies the horse. "Nothing speaks for itself. Not even words …," and pausing a moment, he adds, "… or odd ones, for that matter."

"Absolute ventriloquy is the condition of existence because there's a kind of general expressivity or, as some would say, physiognomic significance in the form of things that makes their *appearances* exchangeable[13]—the things themselves aren't exchangeable but the sense for which they stand is, a sense that is felt as a quality rather than recognized as a function."[14]

"How do you know this?" I ask.

"Because it comes straight from the horse's mouth," says the horse, "and if you've been paying attention, then you'll understand that my mouth is your mouth," I say.

"Or at least I thought I said this," I think to myself.

… If absolute ventriloquy is the law, then irony is the rule, and mine can't be its own voice but only a voice whose drawl shares its expressive force with the way lingering tobacco and vanilla notes express the finish of a small-batch bourbon.

Yet if it's all a tape recording, does any of this really matter? Irony is lost when it's forgotten that it's not the opposite of what it's playing at. Irony becomes a law rather than a rule when the ironic gesture inducts us into a register of existence where what matters is no longer what one does but what one's doing stands for. And as a law, irony can no longer exclude the middle. The instantaneous back-and-forths between logical levels that ruled the exchange between contrastive terms no longer holds when "It is all recorded" because there is no point of view that is not already what it is not.[15] In other words, under the law of irony everything is impossible to exchange.

However, if I'm okay with lying to myself, then maybe there's no problem. When everything says something that does not denote what those sayings for which they stand would denote, all I need is a little superstition. Well, actually, I need a little *hyper*stition. Superstition really only helps me navigate a reality that's seemingly above my control because when I'm superstitious I'm just trying to *seduce* results from something I think is beyond my grasp. But when I'm too much in control of my reality—like when "It is all recorded"—*Nothing* is beyond my expression of it. This means that I have to create *Nothing*; I have to invent an occasion of inexplicability, not in order to break the law that "It is all recorded," but to *alienate* results from actions or, rather, to estrange effects from causes. Like a dream whose verisimilitude subsists in the ignorance of its similitude, being hyperstitious gives me a way to instrumentalize the truth of irony by making it lie, which, in a sense, makes it meaningful. In other words, being hyperstitious is a weird kind of pragmatism, one that lets me take my bullshit seriously.

There is no band, yet I hear a band. And someone is singing a familiar song, but I don't know the words. I'm crying and there's a horse telling me that he likes to play. Hands take my wrist and fingers softly trace the poetry of a well-worn tragedy along my arm. A poem—the sensation is like a lullaby. It makes me drowsy. *J'entends le parti pris des choses*, and I begin to dream it wasn't real. It was all a tape recording.

4

Psycho(tic)acoustics

(E)S

Last night I dreamed that celebrated Russian neuropsychologist Alexander Luria's equally famous patient, known as S, was once again expressing dismay at the entailments of his hypermnesic condition. As is well known, a particular side effect of his photographic memory rendered him unable to accumulate snapshots, *shadings* of an object, into a graspable whole with finite boundaries, an operation Husserl called adumbration. Most notably, S could not collapse the various faces of an individual into a coherent, phenomenologically and conceptually solid syndrome known as a person, which vexed him to no end.

This time, however, S was complaining about a newer, sonic symptom characterized by an incapacity to gather segments of a remembered piece of music into a resolved entity that could be accessed in its totality, such that a desired passage could be swiftly pinpointed without having to submit to real-time audition. S claimed to have discovered this supplementary deficit when attempting recollection of Erik Satie's *Gnossienne #6*.

As he described the obsessional nature of listening internally to music that yielded no quarter to either repetition or difference, both operating infra-legibly, I began to hear it too. This wasn't a type of hypermnesia I was acquainted with. Impossibly, the music constantly folded into itself, perpetually reprising, yet never stopping in order to actually begin again. Rather than flatly looping, it secreted a loop-effect while remaindering a curious intuition of difference, slipping constant variation beneath detection capabilities. This Satie derivation inhabited a strange parasitic middle, refusing straight capture by mnemonic processes yet constantly leveraging the accretion of fractal similes against a gradual habituation to its averaged-out contours.

Perhaps Satie's music was already *anadumbratively* disposed. I recalled being stupefied by Johnny Mandel's "rearrangement" of the French iconoclast's *Gnossienne #5* for the 1979 film *Being There*, a bait-and-switch the full import of which only became apparent oneirically. In that dream, Mandel's unsubtle quantizations of the original's prickly rhythmic irregularities and gross ablation of its chromatic countenance underwent further exacerbation, shamelessly trading stoic impenetrability for homespun emotiveness.

While the vagaries of copyright circumvention might provide tractable insights into the shadowy realm of anadumbration, this was most assuredly far from S's immediate concern. He believed himself to be trapped in what he called a "chronic templex," dejectedly adrift in an absurd, anti-cumulative topology, as if tethered to a permutational algorithm perfectly tailored to his mnemonic affordances, whose output always lay just out of digestible range. S couldn't extract the invariant melodic, harmonic, rhythmic elements from the experience and pinch them into a bounded unit, which made him immune to the exploits of sonic branders who appreciate the advantages of adroitly gaming incongruity thresholds so that a sign is able to retain its integrity as it is encountered in dispersed fashion across multiple scales, spaces, and temporalities.

In a previous dream, S had related another, eminently anadumbrative maladaptation involving an inaptitude at recognizing an already heard song by virtue of its differential circumstances of enactment. He remembered every iteration in excruciatingly resolved detail, each composed of complex feedback relationships between acoustics (indoor or outdoor, inflected by temperature and humidity), contingent human and nonhuman action, fortuitous abutments (an aberrant hummer on the tram ride home from work), his own physical and psychic states, synchronous attunements, and other situational factors. S progressively came to grips with the idea that each new song jotted down in his notation pocketbook for future recollection—hypomnemata were his friends, guarding him against mutation intolerance—was already ensconced in its pages, note for note.

A speculative program charged with defeating identity formation and the perceptual straitjackets of time-binding could do worse than hijack S's anadumbrative complexion. Crystallizations of behavior, personality, categories of experience—and their transmission to the future—all depended on a stalwart model of chronological time, scripted into the organism at the most basic level, ably abetted by the irreversible linearity of language. Music's slacker engagement with causal narrative and logical progression occasionally masked its equally fatal addiction to one-way temporality, which made it an ideal medium to prototype unbinding technologies.

Anadumbration requires astute calibration to the auditory distribution of a given spacetime and its particular scaling of difference and repetition. Moreover, given networked feedback's endless reconfigurational proclivities, it cannot but function diagrammatically, playing relations over positions. Branders understood relational invariance all too well, which is why anadumbration parasitically insinuates itself within the shapeshifting procedures that rely on it, dissolving the constraints that guarantee an entity its integrity, instead fostering an indefinite leakage of its mutational potentials. And though the phenomenon portrayed herein occurs primarily on melodic and harmonic levels, rhythmic, timbral, and dynamic anadumbrations can be easily envisaged.

PR(DBS)

Anadumbration's mission to loosen the strictures of time necessitates a prior confrontation with formalisms that ratify the boundaries conditioning the extent of possible variation. Peter Roehr—a German artist intuitively attuned to the serpentine powers of repetition, key to the infiltrational enterprise—and his close confidant Danel B. Scroll had been acquainted with a now-disappeared tract from 1965 entitled *Kapital Verinnerlicht* (Capital Internalized). The pamphlet—simply ascribed to "Anonymus"—was precocious in its depiction of the tentacular monstrosity of capital, bent on destruction in order to more efficiently pursue accumulation into the remotest regions of everyday life. As Scroll tersely elucidated (in a rare statement), "Capital is inseparable from daily experience. It is immanent to its nuclear specifics." Indeed, Scroll and Roehr preemptively gleaned what many others subsequently missed: grotesque capital and its consummate shapeshifting skills already fully inhabited the supposedly incalculable human vitalities in excess of it, which rendered futile any productive possibility of resistance from a vantage external to its infective ministrations.

Recognizing the dependence of capitalist predation on the minutiae of its delivery vehicles—its Vodun servitors—both took to the molecular infra road, committing themselves to minimalist appropriationist programs that would operate from the inside out.

That same year, Roehr secured both filmed and radiophonic commercials gathered by his partner Paul Maenz from his advertising job in New York in order to infuse himself with "die Rhythmen des Kapitals." By excising a segment from one of them and ouroborically splicing its extremities together, he formed a loop that, on playback, initiated what he called a *movement-network*, a delicate configuration with a peculiar half-life. At first, he noticed how the loop differentially apportioned its informational content over a range of iterations, marveling at the magical "appearance" of elements that had always been there, which unerringly distracted from the equally uncanny ebbing of once prominent features.

But after constructing a number of these closed circuits and immersing himself in their logics, Roehr began to understand that he was really investigating occult forms of entrainment, the loops ferreting out the limits of a distribution of the sensible that operated proficiently but stealthily, its ambit habitually occluded. These weird obsessive-compulsive life hacks—technologies of the self—enabled a grasping of operations usually out of reach, and therefore inalienable.

Though Roehr keenly apprehended repetition's astonishing knack for collapsing an assemblage of phenomena, however complex and heterogeneous, into a bound thing, it took the auditioning of a hackneyed conversation to propel this insight further. As iterations progressed, he noticed how the semantic content of the speech began to capitulate to its purely sonic carrier, until he caught himself humming the melody that eventually stabilized. The principle of semantic satiation and its concomitant promotion of pitch salience had shepherded a remarkable and irreversible transmutation, yet the loop matter itself remained stolidly invariant.

There was more. Through this becoming-aphasic, integral to musicalization, the newly reified entity lent itself to exact, verbatim retention, thereby operationalized for future recall and use. In effect, Roehr found himself able to intone the melody henceforth with considerable ease. It was unsplittable. A fragment thereof could not be cleanly extracted without occasioning integral replay, confirming the ubiquity of time-binding.

Crucially, Roehr discovered that progressive tunneling into the molecular microstructures of the organism eventually forced retention itself to switch modalities. A cognitively valenced, routinized schema typical of longer, syntactical processes was jettisoned in these loop experiments for a ritualized, goal-demoted form tethered to motor functions.

Finally, repetition's inevitable amplification of activity in the emotional centers of the brain sealed the compact, activating a participatory entrainment, a listening as a doing, a feeling of ownership of an aggregate that shackled the listener ever more tightly to its rhythms and associations. Fueled by the dopamine insurgency accompanying this appropriation, an individual's sense of available agency could be punctually reset. Launching a particular movement-network seemed to guarantee both a boost in confidence and improved efficiency. One of them forced itself into every available temporal niche within his daily ritual, entraining him to perform his ablutions, walk to the market, and prepare dinner in accordance with its recursive cadences.

Roehr fathomed the dark side of a giddy infatuation with self-modulators, anticipating the later proliferation of earworms. As the film *Inception* illustrated, capture is more effective if one believes oneself to be the originator of an idea rather than its unsuspecting medium of incubation. In need of empirical data, he auditioned both film and sound loops for friends—focus groups—in order to determine the threshold beyond which the repeated bundle bifurcated into a qualitatively different state, as if implicated in a catastrophe diagram. Roehr verified the extent of a sequence's binding by periodically cutting the sound before completion of an iteration, deftly dropping entrainment checks into the session. Holes are endemically parasitic, demanding constant infill by their unwitting hosts. While the experiments were initially tasked with gauging the approximate number of repetitions required to achieve protentional satiation—the movement-network's resting phase in thermodynamic terms, when expectations are zeroed out—something more insidious was called for. He used the opportunity to determine the termination point in each concatenation that would most optimally ensure mental completion, confirming secure binding. Evidence was scant, except for one instance in which the becoming-musical of a speech sequence induced remanent humming—at the precise pitch level of the original—after Roehr had aborted playback.

At a time in which listening is radically dispersed along an uncountable plethora of incommensurate vectors, the ability to accurately track exposure to repeated signals inevitably cedes to chronic cryptomnesia. Unknown knowns. Imagine S, blithely unaware of his level of acclimatization to a particular tune, pummeled by a quantum increase in subliminal reinforcements. Indeed, occulted repetition has the effect of stealthily intensifying an entity's qualia so that a song you once hated can suddenly become appealing. Anything could be naturalized under the aegis of the demon of repetition. Fictions circulating ubiquitously—and recessively—möbiusoidally ratified into immutable facts, with no one the wiser.

An anadumbrative exploit seeking to defeat such perilous crystallizations would have to account for the thickness of engagement the sequence affords over time—its habituation circuit—approximating its complexity-leveling catastrophic thresholds to forestall an unwanted redoubling of its mnemonic fortitude.

DM

Hyperstition is a social technology charged with the transmutation of fictions into realities, inducing materialized effects via the insinuation of inscrutable, yet strategically designed attractors into feedback systems. Practitioners keenly grasp its capacity to sidestep the paradoxical machinations of resistant noise, which, in the manner of deprogramming sessions, actively reinstantiates—retroproduces—that which it seeks to dispose of by rational argumentation. Indeed, noise is indispensable to an advanced cybercapitalist ecology, periodically regenerating it through its interventions and thereby marshaling increasingly robust immunization against unaffordable experience. Rather than submitting to this eternal game of catch-up, a hyperstitional probehead functions parasitically through misconstrual, surfacing latent formalisms and affective modalities that subtend what can be thought, while obliquely recoding them. With no immediate basis to safely contain it, the probehead ratchets a system's internal logics into legibility according to the singular rhythms of the cargo cult contagion.

Declan Morl, a barrister by day and mnemonist in his spare time, ran a literary salon in London in the mid-1930s that occasionally hosted "transmutational listening séances." He particularly favored the game of Pareidolatry, which, as its portmanteau coinage intimates, was dedicated to inculcating a slavish devotion through persuasive patterning. A typical session involved the playback of a musical work pervasively accompanied by Morl's narration, a motley assemblage of absurdly detailed phenomenal annotations cunningly coupled with incongruous but equally fastidious descriptions of other musics and faux-historical contextualizations.

What might have come off as an intractable hodgepodge of discrepant verbiage was ably congealed by Morl's considerable hortatory skill honed in his professional life, already appreciably enhanced by his resonant baritone. These were both indispensable in the induction of self-fulfilling prophecies, goading listeners to hear things that were absent from the acoustic signal, perceptual and cognitive chimeras that nevertheless registered as absolutely real. In point of fact, the origin of these experiments lay in an account related by one of Morl's associates who had recently emerged from deafness into an inchoate world that *could not be heard* for its lack of discursive embedding.

For all that, Morl approached his revisionist recounting conservatively at first, traveling within restricted confines he felt would guarantee commitment from his devotees. Plagued by the fear that one clumsily managed transition could fell the byzantine scaffolding, assembled piecemeal, he resorted to elementary tactics: the anachronic misattribution of a work to another author—ofttimes historically subsequent, entailing an amusing disordering of stylistic periodization—or a Heraclitean potentiation of weak emissions, wherein peripheral details were magnified into centrality, a phenomenon familiar to Roehr.

(Proceedings weren't always aboveboard. Morl's intermittent loss of nerve led him to conceal a second phonograph playing back at relatively subliminal levels the music(s) at the origin of the projective instructions, earning him the nickname "Declined Morals.")

His comrade's testimony nagged at him as the sessions evolved. If the simple act of identification resulted in audibility, why not scale up the endeavor and conjure formations that resided fully outside of the phonographic inscription, springing them into palpability? Scrapping the vestiges of realistic description, Morl quickly confirmed that the most outrageously incongruous concoctions actually cemented adherence, such that whatever occurred after them was accepted wholesale. It seemed that a tell-tale heart lurked in the occult core of every hyperstitional gambit: an indigestible, unabsorbable fiction that sent listening into panic mode, the only way out of which was through hallucination. The apophenic propensities ascribed to Konstantīns Raudive and his fellow Electronic Voice Phenomena researchers were only a minor subset of a generalized delusional predicament part and parcel of a human aversion to untenable irrationality. The signal-to-noise ratio could be restructured on the fly, with a few judiciously deployed statements, leaving the signal itself intact but its perceptualization irrevocably altered. You can never return to chaotic equivocation once fatally spiked by the powers of the false.

Morl's efforts at probing the pliability of audition when subjected to motivational myths affords valuable insights into hyperstitional functionality. Reality potency is only a function of relative consistency, internal to a carefully constructed story. Infinitely malleable surface dynamics invariably trump ontological guarantees. Recall Reagan's welfare queen diatribe designed to render inevitable the dismantling of social security. The left brain's narrative infilling capacities—secondary processes, in Freudian terminology—complete the circuit, papering over residual inconsistencies. It is immaterial whether the fiction's constitutive elements happen to coincide with any existing reality, the latter altogether provisionalized in the name of pragmatic engagement rather than epistemological hesitation. Acting *as if* one is rational effectively ratifies all manner of irrationality, as the economist Gary Becker grasped.

Anadumbrators, like magicians, had to be masters of attention management, adept at modulating the tactility of temporal perception by calibrating protentions and retentions. The engineering of expectation and especially its thwarting were key to maintaining the listener in a state of emotional intoxication. Wasn't it James who noted that "articulate reasons are cogent for us only when our inarticulate feelings of reality have already been impressed in favor of the same conclusion?"

Morl's occult pareidolatry irresistibly opened onto a wide expanse of exoteric implications. In George Kubler's circuit model of history, phenomena are never completely exhausted, perpetually relaying into the future signals insufficiently strong to register at their inceptive moment but that gain prominence when eventually linking up with an appropriate historical conjuncture. Imagine time-traveling, data-mining robots from a not-so-distant future—revalencing machines—that perform ever-higher resolution revisionist analyses of the past as correlational techniques gain in speed and efficiency. Nebulous discrepancies, anonymous to each other, become punctually aligned through the magnetic pull of such an exogenous, alien force. Hyperstition is just that reconfiguring, templexing spanner that preempts conventional historical processes in order to instantiate statistically improbable lines of investigation, rewiring perception while making plain the utter relativity and convulsive mutability of any regime of signification. Like Valéry's anonymous surfers of literary combinatoriality—now endowed with awesome computational power—hyperstitionists regard chronological history as a fetishized conceit that can be bent and remade at will. What dormant valences await their present reckoning, unleashed via a retrodeposited story from the future?

DBS(PR)

After Roehr's premature death, Scroll ran with his bare formulations, convinced that the repetition-binding scheme compelled further intensification and implementation on a grander scale. With the help of a rudimentary recording system first installed in his apartment and then taken out into the world, he captured segments of varying length documenting the rhythms of everyday life that were then looped over headphones or reinjected into his living room via loudspeakers. Scroll believed the maniacally graduated ergonomics characteristic of early twentieth-century time and motion studies had metastasized beyond the factory into a method of subliminal social regulation at large, and therefore sought to expose the frameworks subjugating movement to rigid temporal quantization.

Perpetual looping spawned unintended effects. A draconian overuse of compression grossly reduced the dynamic compass of the signal, amplifying background rhythms into cognizance and attenuating foreground activity, effectively collapsing both onto the same perceptual plane. An epileptic, Scroll was captivated by the trance-like templexes fomented by an overattentiveness to micro-events, which increased in duration and magnitude until he could no longer selectively attend to crucial stimuli nor disregard low-level ritualizations. He had preemptively reached a state all too familiar to contemporary humans, hyperpermeated by informational vectors and increasingly incapable of distinguishing epiphanic synchronicities from apophenic, pareidolic phantasms. Reality has itself become paranoiac, overfolded mud, slackened by too many connections. Moreover, the obsessiveness with which Scroll attended to his loops ineluctably invoked the musicalizing appetites of repetition probed by Roehr, thereby overwhelming his amygdala, the neuroemotional nexus especially activated by music. With too much affective stuff to dispose of, Scroll withdrew into quasi-autistic confinement. His life hack had möbiusoidally mutated into a life hijack.

Roehr's phonographic concretions functioned synecdochically, entraining the body into a trajectory against which the passing of time could be apprehended and judiciously tracked. Scroll's deficiencies significantly liberated him from the consolidating compulsions of time, affording him unsuspected advantages. Aided by the leveling tendencies of compression that brought heterogeneous elements into adjacent range, Scroll began work on *Nebenformeln* ("nearby formulas")[*], a combinatorial modality governing the superimposition of fragments, eventually songs that, bound together once, would remain associated in perpetuity through the industrious workings of repetition.

Like Morl, Scroll was bewitched by the manifold methods of restructuring acoustic fields, ultimately devoting himself to syzegetic combines for their defiantly arcane attributes. In these double earworms, each component remained accessible, yet fatally intertwined with the other. Such imbrication was accomplished through psychoacoustic principles like masking, in which the spectral components of one song temporarily overwhelm the other, redirecting listening; and metamorphosis, an insidious operator concealing the emergences and disappearances of either song, clinching indivisibility.

Devoid of analytical cutting or editing, these constructs observed more topological modalities. Scroll's physical condition may have intensified his sensitivity to interval sizes and contours, given the processing of the latter via the temporal lobe, an area subjected to frequent seizures. The

---

[*] The awkwardness of this term reflects Scroll's average command of German, which he did not speak fluently. Something more akin to *Adjazenzformeln* (adjacency formulas) was probably what he had in mind.

glischroid temperament comorbid with epilepsy attuned him to the relative viscosity of particular overlays, a stickiness both expediting song binding and improving its circulatory traction once unleashed into the world. To boot, he suspected his mutant graftings might induce *vampire effects*—anathema to sonic branders—that could permanently deep-six the effective currency of a song or fraction thereof.

It behooves me to address the esoteric origins of these adjacencies, lest one think them purely the product of a strategic interventionist demeanor. Indeed, long before the *Nebenformeln* became subject to conceptual attention, Scroll had been hallucinating phantom tunes that superimposed themselves without effort onto songs playing back in the air. The naturalness of the phenomenon alerted him to the possibility that some form of closure was under way, a weird variant of the psychoacoustical axiom describing an automatic propensity to internally complete a heard pattern. He accepted his destiny as the recipient of a challenge-response interaction, the spectral completing the physically sounded, though the ultimate stakes of this rejoinder remained wholly cryptic.

On October 28, 1978, after many years of hermetic isolation, Scroll hallucinated Elton John's "Daniel" while Billy Joel's just released "My Life" was playing on the radio, immediately before experiencing a powerful temporal lobe seizure. The event—decoded by "My Life" five years, seven months, and two days after the release of "Daniel"—impelled a final epiphanic statement in the form of a published score of "Daniel" overlaid with a transparent sheet on which the pitches and rhythms of "My Life" had been meticulously notated, in sync. The message received, Scroll returned to his self-imposed retreat, though his amalgamating intuitions remained potent. Having recently been unexpectedly accosted by "Daniel" in a department store, I could not help but hear "My Life" folded in, lined up exactly as it had been in Scroll's parasitic compound.

The Psychosonic Anarchist Detail (PSAD) developed an eponymous app in homage to Scroll's formulas, a spontaneous vampirizer détourning the popular tune-recognition system Shazam by hijacking its code. Upon detecting song playback, PSAD trawls through Shazam's dataset to locate, as per specified parameters, another tune to latch to it in perfect synchronicity, infecting anyone in the vicinity. The hacked app's abilities to algorithmically pinch together subcutaneous invariances, thereby conjoining previously discrepant surfaces, announce the inexorable dissolution of prevailing categorical segregations. Moreover, because they function as psychic ergonomics—transitional, flexible scaffoldings for the production of extended minds—apps of this ilk can assiduously administer varieties of quantum modulation well beyond the dreams of Muzak's inventors.

C(EA)G

An attempt to conjure such a distributed mind was carried out in an experiment entitled *Carpenter et al. Downey Lyrical Holdings, a Real-Time Social System, as of March 29, 2007*. Machinically extracted fragments culled from the Carpenters' integral song repertoire—chosen for its prodigious earworm-spawning intelligence—are externalized by two musicians receiving them over headphones and taken up by several sets of players, each operating according to different filtration modalities specifying listening orientation and consequent response. The *spinners* (or *entrainers*) at the inception of the cycle are tasked with learning these randomly generated slivers on the spot and progressively congealing them together, synthesizing their jagged incompatibilities into a melodically continuous, repeatable whole. Their efforts, coalescing over fits and starts, replete with mishearings and erroneous translations, constitute the already distorted material that the *diffusers* (the second group) appropriate and extend through further melodic divagation and controlled extemporization. The *splitters*, on the other hand, privy to the inceptive fragments (which are never actually heard in the room) attempt their precise replication, inevitably abutting against instrumental limitations fostering additional, contingent mutation. As this third and final group enters, the spinners receive a fresh set of sound bites that initiates another cycle, intercalating new material into the folds of the ongoing process.

What begins as a relatively linear chain of influence and mimicry soon metastasizes into a cloud of contaminating feedback that slowly acquires an autonomous character, while unceasingly modulated by its constituent members whose discrete interventions are dynamically gauged relative to discernable effects on the evolving entity. The interpenetration of quantum perspectives on singular particles looses the fetters keeping lines in time, gradually depriving them of their causal solidity and inevitability. Earworm-packets hierarchically organized by network protocols reassemble into units that, as per a Jamesian mosaic, associate, conflate, and concatenate into heretical formations with unpredictable potential.

This egregor—the Vodun emergent intelligence described here—materializes as a result of differentially articulated scripts, inflected by an unstable mix of paranoia and enthusiasm, intentional acts of collective adhesion and unintended collusions, mass entrainments whose summed resonances sporadically induce structural collapse. Music is conscripted for its capacities to organize and simulate coordination over its individualizing, conservative entrapments typically dedicated to promoting embodied security, temporal sanctity, and attendant conceptions of order. Moreover, a coherent self can no longer be feasibly sustained, adrift in the vortical, cybernetic channels of febrile teleplasty (morphing at a distance). *I know where I am, but I do not feel as though I'm on the spot where I find myself.* The mimic's assimilation to her mutating surroundings and ego dissolution are conventionally marked as thanatropic, psychotic dispositions. For the hyperstitionist, such anonymization—becoming-background—is the sine qua non of effective infiltration.

Access is primordial, origins immaterial. Syndromes of interlocking processes are passed along, fleetingly constituting and just as soon dismantling quasi-objects and quasi-subjects, all the while simulating systemic, epistemological, and morphological protocols. As the exploratory probehead pings a social context's pattern distributions and its dominant egregors, it sets into motion a cargo cult scenario, in which the relation with the alien object is slowly erased in favor of foregrounding the internal relations of the group, increasingly complexified and destabilized by that which it cannot conceptually stomach. In a distinctly anadumbrative gait, the search for additional dimensions to ratify initial impressions only results in a further deferral of secure closure.

In *Being There*, Peter Sellers, a consummate cipher, assumes the identity of a simpleminded man whose every anodyne utterance is immediately interpreted as evidence of epigrammatic, allegorical insight, quickly sweeping him into proximity with political power and mass media. It is a classic case of hermeneutic serendipity, familiar to any hyperstitionist. Indeed, a finer carrier than Chance the Gardener could scarcely be envisioned, an alien agent (for whom walking on water is a matter of course) unintentionally restructuring social dynamics in spiraling magnitudes, simply by dint of ubiquitous mirroring and a default phraseology.

Sellers, who admitted to lacking a true self, was accordingly pathologized within a quaintly antiquated paradigm that could not admit the opportunities for experimental forms of corporeal and cognitive action flowing from the failure to build up a personality. The psychasthenic's inability to produce her limits of being or bind time, though negatively valenced, is simply symptomatic of a broader conception of the individual as pervasively porous and amorphous, a thoroughly provisional syndrome composed of multiple symbiotic organisms without readily ascertainable beginnings or endings.

PS

The emblematic composite whence this narrative sprang must have occurred in a flash: the anonymous probehead Sellers—or S—transfixed by a TV exercise program, the sum total of his worldly knowledge collated from the tube's endless proliferation of predigested, already bound units, mimicking the performer's movements to the anadumbrated airs of Satie's *Gnossienne #6*, sporadically lapsing into Mandelian redolence. It was a peerless consolidation, evoking Scroll's most glutinous contrivances.

I had planned on awakening from my nap pursuant to the familiar prompts: a workout video from the 1980s whose cheerful patterning usually managed to cut into oneiric activity, backed up in case of failure by a hydraulic pump charged with elevating the footrest of my chair until I toppled over. In fact, I did wake up, but into a wholly other setting, a control room of sorts operated by the spitting image of Jack Lemmon... But that's another story.

5
The sound of both ears oozing: Chasms, collapses, and phono-digital networks

Last night I dreamed of mud, oozing from my ears. I'm lying prostrate on my belly with my eyes closed and there is a weird and dolorous melody meandering in the background. The experience recalls Steven Connor's beautifully written account of tinnitus, wherein he describes the condition as one of "intercepting [his] own hearing processes, listening in on the work of [his] own ears."[1] This amounts, for Connor, to a kind of auto-interceptive listening where the intra-hearing feedback loop is characterized as an informational black box. We know what goes in and what comes out, but "we do not know precisely what happens in the middle."[2] Moreover, since it is *auto*-interceptive it might be more accurate to say that we know there are transformative comings and goings, but we do not know the direction of the transformations nor specifically what they entail. And indeed, these oto-acoustic emissions—these sounds produced by the ear that interact with the "outside" acoustic world but that are not *of* either—are not exclusive to listeners living with tinnitus. They are instead a constitutive component of listening in general that is made explicit in the case of tinnitus.

My oneiric ears, muddied as they are, thus introduce a certain sensitivity to the relationality of listening that tinnitus suggests, and also (reflexively) to the inattentional injunction that nontinnital listening can entail with respect to relations. That is, listening is always muddy, but sometimes you have to get your ears dirty to tune into just what this means, and all the more so in a time when relations are understood as neutral conduits that convey information between data points (i.e., via a communication model). In contrast to such determinations, I dream of a mucilage-inflected hearing that intensifies a tinnital vector, where a "vector can be thought of as any material form a relation can take which has certain definable qualities but which has no fixed position."[3] Put simply, my auralneiric muddiness attests to the sonic systematicities that are produced by the relationality of a (not necessarily human) listening that defies being diagrammed according to its signals, senders, and receivers. The mud is at once the source of my partial deafness and an amplifier of the sounds of my listening.

Thus, though I might well indulge in the pleasures of an auscultation-through-mire in a way that approaches musical listening—where the point would be to find what is present in the world and make music out of that, in the manner of Cage—the sound/nonsound threshold that is chiefly characteristic of that listening is slightly awry. A sound includes not only the many components issuing from, say, a violin, "but all of the incidental vibration that already animates the space, waiting to be modulated to the point of audibility by a suitable sound."[4] That is, musical listening is a technique that fosters (and is fostered by) (non)sound, an extra-sonorous "semblance of aliveness that appears in sound."[5] And indeed, one can posit such cultivation as constitutive of listening in general insofar as the latter is understood as a kind of operation that is catalyzed by sounds, but one that is not coextensive with them. This being the case, music functions rhetorically rather than ontologically vis-à-vis sound, specifically articulating it in its technological aspect: it helps us to understand what the organization of sound *produces*.

With my ears full of sludge, though, this extra-sonorous nonsonic sound that comes with listening takes hold in a different way. If musical listening—and the listening in general that flows from it, and back toward it—points to a threshold between sound and nonsound at the level of production, then listening with mud slopping about in my ears is a kind of nonlistening where production and reception are no longer even provisionally separable. In this dream, the muddy relationality precedes the component parts it purportedly causes, in that the relations are (in a reverse causality) produced in their particularity as much as they are uncovered as components of a listening system. Pondering this, I am jerked briefly into consciousness, palpated by the palindrome flashing from the clock: 2:22 ... presumably AM.

Lying still, still, in bed, my ears seeping, I realize that the metaphor of a threshold in the sound/nonsound relation is replaced in my experience by that of a *texture*, where the suffix -ure indicates "something that results from" and where *text* in this instance traces its etymology to "weaving." *Texture*, then, is somewhat apocryphal, standing in for a kind of qualitative shift like that of a mixture, where the component parts are no longer separable. The difference here, however, is that a sonic texture's component parts (sound and nonsound) are not found anywhere else, so that, in this formulation, we are discussing a texturing of ongoing effects rather than an object per se: a texturing of the real material effects of ideal objects. It's a texturing of a vector, which is a queer sort of mixture: a recursive textured vector in and of itself.

To speak clearly—even if I can't be sure I'm hearing myself correctly—my muddy dream modulates the question of listening to emphasize (to my ears, at least) a position outside the individual listener. This is ironic, given that the muddiness came to me through the experience of a dream, a mode of experience that is more personal than the personal. Nonetheless, it calls me to hear listening as occurring in a space that is already full: the space of my listening brims over like an incoming tide, not just obscuring the shoreline but in fact redrawing it (both intensively within and extensively beyond myself).

To put it schematically: if listening as texture indelibly mixes the productive and receptive vectors of listening by conceiving the space of the listening apparatus (in my case, my ears) as full to the point of overflowing, and if this emphasizes the oto-acoustic dimension of listening, then in order to extend this framework beyond the individual listener one need only conceive of the listening apparatus more broadly: to surf the muddy flow. And indeed, any material analysis of listening would attest to the fact that such an expansion has always already occurred through the distended temporalities and spatialities that sever all sounds from their sources and destinations (i.e., that make sound sound), and all the more so through the technical intensification of sound's extensivity that comes about with the full-blown rhizophonia of contemporary recording and digital networks.[6]

The reference already seems dated, but we might say that this is a shift from thinking about sounds as *a movement into us* toward thinking of them as *occupying* and thereby reshaping us: a movement, after all, aims for internal consistency but uses space "just as a place to park its ranks," whereas an occupation has no internal consistency but "chooses meaningful spaces that have significant resonance into the abstract terrain of symbolic geography."[7] That is, sound particularizes in individual bodies such that it occupies the abstract space through which those bodies relate, which is to say, the intervals, tempos, intensities, amplitudes, contours, and boundaries through which they become bodies in the first place. A sound makes no demands except to be heard.

Put differently, there is what one might call a "primary relationality" to listening that suggests the black box not just as a problem for communication, but in fact as the problematic form of communication itself: the form through which an informatic paradigm wherein relations are mere connections—indifferent to their content, and qualitatively equivalent—is denaturalized. This, then, is listening to communication as noncommunication, which is also to suggest the possibility of an arche-listening... or perhaps not: this is after all a dream I'm discussing, and if nothing else, we know that a dream is never about exactly what it seems, precisely because the separation that is implicit in the word "about" precludes such immanence. The thought of this separation hits me and I briefly jolt awake, rattled by the clamor of the palindrome on the clock: 3:33... presumably AM.

Lying still, still, though tensely, I'm resolutely *not* making a claim about what sound or listening is, but rather experiencing a way in which sound's texturing capacity mobilizes a specific form of *networking*, a specific way of thinking relations. I'm not motivated in this particular present (tense) situation from my auralneiric past, but I am as I write this now because it moves toward engaging a substantial challenge of our time and place that Anna Munster terms "network anaesthesia." The nomination denotes the prominence that the nodes-and-edges-style diagram has gained in describing relations in our era of computer network technologies. With the phrase "network anaesthesia," then, Munster names "a numbing of our perception that turns us away from [networks'] unevenness and from the varying qualities of their relationality."[8] Put simply, virtually every available image of a network is a variation of the nodes-and-edges form, and this form of diagram occludes the specifics of the relations it represents in favor of a generalized notion of interaction.

It is no accident that this form comes to such prominence in the context of late global capitalism, when exchangeability itself is not changed by what is exchanged. In this respect, capital and information are isomorphic and together limn a mediatic form that technically specifies knowledge in our time as sited in relata that not only precede their relations but are also not qualitatively affected by them. Thus, as Munster puts it, "what we have lost... is the *experience* of the edges, the experience of relation."[9] From this observation, Munster takes seriously William James's injunction that "the relations that connect experiences must themselves be experienced relations."[10] If, as McKenzie Wark argues, "any social form resides within a communication infrastructure that gives it a certain shape, a certain tempo [that renders the infrastructure at least] somewhat invisible,"[11] then Munster's point is simply that this problem is intensified through its reenactment in contemporary technoculture. This is particularly the case when, as Mark Hansen argues, for the first time in history media involve "technical operations to which humans lack any direct access,"[12] such that media no longer mediate just a sensory experience that precedes the medium (like, say, an image) but actually also mediate the medium itself, which is to say, the connectivity that comes with our massively distributed extrasensory technical infrastructure.[13]

For the argument I'm trying to incant while I dream—before its inevitable recantation that comes with waking—it is important to note that the problem of network anaesthesia highlights a technical conception of relation, not only in the computational sense but also in the representational frameworks that subtend visualization technologies and the graph theory with which such frameworks commingle. As Munster puts it so eloquently, "the shift from hierarchical to relational data [that characterizes the shift from the Internet as an encyclopedia to the Internet as an interactive framework] is tied into the development of a general network *dispositif* coextensive with an entire social field of 'the network.'"[14] It follows, then, that network anaesthesia is tied up in the affordances and constraints of specific methods of data visualization; and indeed, in visualization itself as a method, since every visualization is at once dependent on its method of excluding and prioritizing data *and* constitutively incapable of representing within its framework that which is excluded or deemphasized in this method. Picturing this paradox, I am briefly prickled awake, irritated by the palindrome on the clock: 4:44… presumably AM.

Lying less still, fidgeting, I can begin to hear how specifically *sonic* texturing might approach this problem. Rather than supplementing the relational anaesthesia of data visualization with sonification (which would, really, just amount to a different experience of the same framework), sonic *texturing*, like that of my dream, revalences established and mature conversations about sound and relations: the refluent soundscape of the churning paste in my ears recalls, for example, the phonochasmic and phonocollapsing activities that Agent RedBreast emphasizes in the arrayed microphone experiments undertaken by Glenn Gould in the mid-70s. In essence, the term phonochasm describes the "[severing of a] subject from its acoustical milieu, delivering it into schizophonic chaos through a judicious control of reverberation."[15] Gould's experiments in this direction involved, as RedBreast describes, "the alignment of an array of microphone pairs extending from the interior of the piano ... to the back of the hall, allowing for cinematic zooming away from and into the musical *object* of attention [and] constant shuttling between an intimate closeness devoid of context to an overpowering of the putative signal by its resonant effects."[16] In short, if schizophonia aims to describe a psychic condition that arises from a culture wherein sounds are consistently separated from their sources, phonochasms are the material conditions that execute this.

Phono*collapses,* then, are in one sense antipodal to phonochasms on the phonic continuum, describing a condition of an undifferentiated whole: an object case, for example, might be audio recorded on a Ferguson protester's mobile phone in the chaotic scramble to an undefined and undesignated safe location while under a hail of the police's rubber bullets. The constitutive noisiness of such recordings is, of course, not anti-informational but rather precisely informative of a certain context, a context that when pushed to its extreme (as in the case described) reverses into a wild immanence of context collapsing into itself.

RedBreast accentuates the *reverberative* conditions of this continuum, calling for "robust reverb management" both as a recording technique and, more importantly, as a political technique that can include reinjections of reverb in order to promote particularly fertile political vectors.[17] But reverberation is by no means the only technique for moving along the phonochasmic/collapsing continuum, with analogous effects (with different potentials) available through the use of lags, glitches, replacements, and frequency attenuations and amplifications, and through relative emphasis on sound in relation to the other senses. With respect to the latter, for example, Garth Paine recently described to me his use of the Oculus Rift Headset to pair panoramic images of "natural locations" with ambisonic audio of the same places. (Ambisonic audio consists of, basically, a panoramic or spherical recording that is responsive to the movement of the listener's head during playback.) What was remarkable to him (and to me) is that individuals testing the system (including people with a great deal of experience with VR systems) invariably perceived the panoramic still photos to be responsive *videos*. Thus, a leap from a representational interaction to a simulative one is made through a phonocollapse aimed at the visual component of the experience: the suturing of the audio to the contingent movements of the listener's head (many of which movements are autonomic) unhinges the status of the visual interaction.

It should be noted that this phonocollapse is different than what W. J. T. Mitchell calls "braiding," although it follows from it. That is, if braiding names the phenomenon "when one sensory channel or semiotic function is woven together with another more or less seamlessly," the texture of this specific braid is radically singular: the wonder of the pairing doesn't so much lie in the multimediality of the experience, but rather in the way that the *particular* collapse specifies this conjunction such that its medial contexts are no longer independently decipherable.[18] My dream, then, is that approaching sound (momentarily, and contingently) in its texturing capacity allows us to think such phonochasms and collapses in their relationality: my dream is of the muddy texture of phono-digital networks, which is to say, of networks that—in being audible through their (non) sounding—can no longer be thought as informatic statements about the positions of sending and receiving bodies... or even, for that matter, as statements about ontological orders such as representation versus simulation. In short, the texture of the panoramic photo with ambisonic sound is not simulational as opposed to representational; rather, it rubs my muddy ears as an incipient simulationality that is in the lived network that grounds any representational framework.

I'm half awake, taunted by the fleer of the clock's palindrome: 5:55... presumably AM. In my anxiety, I try to capture this dream with a simple, annoyingly literal but fictional example: imagine a project that consists of a series of sound recordings made in Biosphere reserves that are accessible through a website.[19] One goal of such a project might be to map these recordings to GPS coordinates so that they can in turn be superimposed onto a remote listener's physical location using the latter's smartphone. While out for an evening walk, for example, I could listen to a section of the Mojave desert that corresponds in size to the actual distance I'm walking (and, of course, if something catches my ear I could adjust my course and walk toward it). In short, in a manner reminiscent of a Situationist *dérive*, I could map (via a smartphone with headphones) a Biosphere soundscape onto my quotidian surroundings and drift accordingly.

There are many aspects of such a project that I find thought-provoking as I lie awake in bed, larruped by the clock's incessant palindrome: 6:66 ... presumably AM. However, what captures me that day, because of its bald literality, is the relatively novel networking approach that a project like this would take to address a simple technical problem. Put simply, how might one develop a way to move between various ambisonic sound samples without any audible "cuts"? A conventional approach of simply crossfading volumes would introduce a bizarre multiperspectivalism into the ambisonic recordings that—while sounding awesome in its own right—would puncture the integrity of the virtual layer. A different approach to this problem would be to use frequency analysis to stitch together a composite (partially synthetic) network that responds (in "real time") to the listener's movements. The point, in the context of my extrapolated auralneiric experience, is that the latter approach is literally inconceivable within a nodes-and-edges model because the connecting edges would be (in a weird, computational time warp) synthesized as much as they would be uncovered. That is, it's not just that in this fictional example the user's experience of the network would be particularized because they've chosen their own path through the sonic territory, it is also that the sonic territory itself is produced by the relations "uncovered" by the user's pathways. The experience is as much of the unputative relations—of the virtual conjoined sounds that literally exceed their component parts—as it is of the "natural" location that serves as an authenticating alibi.

To reiterate: this is an annoyingly literal example, and it can't really hold my attention away from the moaning, eldritch, red-breasted palindrome flickering on the clock next to me: 7:77...presumably AM. But if it *could*, if I could attend to the mud in my ear's qualities (i.e., its specific productions, amplifications, and attenuations) rather than just understanding it as a signal inhibitor in my hearing process—if I could, that is, develop an aesthesia of networks by attending to relations in their own right—then a significant challenge nonetheless remains in how to make this attention resonant. My wager, in retrospect, is that the phonochasmic-collapse continuum—palpated along tinnital vectors in its extra-reverberative dimensions—might have provided one means of my having done so. It's not the cleanest theoretical approach, and indeed it's more of a theoretical anamnesis...but it nonetheless gurgles in my auralneiric sludge-mind.

6
Motivational dreamers and the 'pataphysics of exploding heads

Last night I dreamed I had my head in the clouds, pillowy shapes taking form as conversations, slowly condensing into heartbeats and metronomes. The clouds spoke to me, sang to me, encouraged me, explained to me where I was and what I was doing, like some strange kind of life coach for an imaginary journey. The clouds had voices—soothing, hypnotic, and persuasive voices—that knew how I was doing, felt my frustrations and aspirations, and monitored my progress as I moved through life. The voices were immersive. I felt them more than heard them, coming from deep inside my head. They were buoyant too, speaking in motivational tones that lifted me to emotional and physical heights. I was dreaming of having my head in the clouds after all, and of having the clouds in my head as well. I awoke with the lingering feeling that I had experienced this relationship before. I quickly realized where: a crowdfunding campaign for a set of smart headphones calibrated to gather performance metrics and provide real-time feedback to the user. The headphones are not on the market yet but are currently being dreamed by engineers, capitalists, and consumers alike, already incorporated into the very fabric of the human imagination, like the clouds during my sleep.

The feedback loop of the story is such as to literally materialize dreams while throwing into question the subjectivity of the dreaming mind. It is a scale shift of sorts: making dreams real and turning reality into its own kind of dream, effectively collapsing the difference between the two, or at least making rhetorical separation contingent on constant relational attention. Swap dreams for virtuality. Adopt analogy as a governing analytic principle. Embrace what sleep researchers call "dream incorporation" as the logic of technological integration. The result is a reversal of the dream phenomenon of "Exploding Head Syndrome," normally understood as the experience of hearing a loud sound at the edge of a dream but in this case just the opposite. The dream makes a loud sound—has a tangible impact—in the material world, and as a result, I begin to realize that I am already being dreamed by machines, even before they are fully invented, motivationally facilitated in ways as much pedagogical as political. We are becoming new subjects of a 'pataphysical regime of smart devices that link us to ourselves in ever more extended and complex ways, digitally rescaling the human imagination in the process.

Motivational dreaming

The device that influenced this dream is not just any device. It was the Bragi Dash, a set of high tech ear buds that connect wirelessly to each other, to any attached peripherals, and to the cloud.[1] They do what any headphones do—they play music—but they also promise new degrees of sonic control over individualized experience: noise-canceling technology that allows for an immersive experience of silence, blocking out all sounds except for the voice of the device itself. They also enable audio transparency if one's preference is to hear everything, overlaying the sounds of the audible world on top of the music. The ear buds contain a microphone that records one's voice through the jaw bone, grabbing the words from the mouth even before they are breathed into the surrounding air and making them digitally transmittable to others. The device also measures body temperature, heart rate, and blood oxygen levels by flashing infrared light beams into the ear to detect minute fluctuations in pulse and air saturation. Taken together, these features provide a robust "bio-mapping" platform that more than satisfies the criteria used in biofeedback geography for calculating a person's emotional state.[2] But on top of all this, the Dash is also an interactive feedback agent, giving real-time spoken input on performance, updating the user on the status of a workout, making suggestions for how one might further optimize activities, and, of course, promising to share all this instantly with one's social network.

But what is so interesting about this device is not just the itemization of technical features but also the promise of emotional and imaginative augmentation—the promise to help us dream a better version of ourselves. Any performance-enhancing technology ostensibly makes this promise, but the Dash does it slightly differently—through sound alone. There is no screen. There is simply a voice inside one's head sharing information about what is happening in one's body and mind. There is an intimacy to this interface, an integration of biometric data and motivational speaking that highlights the ability of sound to augment the transparency of technological integration. This suggests that in the Bragi Dash there is an emergent form of audio reflexivity, a data mirror in the form of a voice that comments and advises on the body's performance in ways that—like the optical mirror before it—shape the fantasy of self and the contingencies of technological identity.

In his book *Exits to the Posthuman Future*, Arthur Kroker meditates provocatively on the new capacity of iPhone technologies to synchronize hearts and smartphones—

reflecting on the biofeedback sensors that allow users to actually send heartbeats (via haptic vibration) to one another in a new language of networked affect.[3] While at first this sort of feature seems like merely a gimmick, for Kroker it can be seen as nothing short of a new language of (emotional) computation. The new generation of wearables has outgrown the idea that electronic brains can only think or analyze or process data: devices now aspire to become fully integrated biological systems. Technology now has a heart—our heart—and as we synchronize with each other in digital embrace, so too do we transform the electronic global brain into a distributed heartbeat. This can be such a smooth transition, Kroker notes, because for the language of computation there is no longer any qualitative difference between the act of measuring and the act of sharing. The ability to share data—to amalgamate and synthesize and evaluate and optimize and broadcast—is already built in to every act of digital measurement. Indeed, part of the social exhilaration with these new distributed parameters lies precisely in the ability to have devices that share our own information back with us, informing us about lives we didn't even know we were leading. Kept in the loop by our own devices. But the device knows it first—knows us more comprehensively than we know ourselves—and that is the part that is a little bit complicated.

To think about it pragmatically, however, is to note that this kind of pervasive broadcast intimacy is really just another symptom of the paradoxical trajectories within which we already live. Media-linked bodies and minds seamlessly juggle feeds of all sorts, from pre-teens mugging the camera on YouTube to cell phone streams of police brutality, from cat videos to Facebook posts, from digital boredom to surveillance anxiety to inspirational motivation in the form of the voices of devices inside our heads. And Kroker's framework is particularly apt, for we live in integrated times, in effect, where all of these things happen all the time, at the same time, in us and around us, all observed and measured, and instantaneously shared.

It would be easy just to say that it seems like a sci-fi dream and to leave it at that, but to push the speculative point would be to try and do one better—actually to try out the language of dreams and see if it works, if it yields some kind of insight or framing device that could be a useful addition to the understanding of technology. For dreams have never been accountable to logic. Rather, dreams often create and sustain narratives despite logic, beginning first with the imperative for an integrated outcome and then amalgamating disparity however necessary in order to hold together the experience. Dreams put complexity first, and in this they have the potential to resonate with the actuality of digital living in ways that more linear or literal forms of understanding might only approximate.

Reality incorporation

The logic of dreams is slippery, however, entwining layers of narrative, affective, and symbolic thought in complex and often surreal ways. Dream researchers refer to this form of logic as "dream incorporation," the method by which real world stimuli are integrated into the experiential narrative of the dreamer.[4] This can happen in traditional psychoanalytic fashion, for example in the way that fear of public embarrassment can provoke anxiety dreams about missing an appointment or forgetting to put on one's pants. But dream incorporation can also be more directly stimulated, integrating physical and perceptual context into a dream as well. The classic stimulus method used in sleep studies is one called "pressure cuff stimulation," in which an inflatable pressurized cuff is placed around the arm or leg of a subject while they sleep. When the subject reaches a state of REM sleep, the researcher inflates the cuff, putting pressure on the physical body of the dreamer. Interestingly, sleeping subjects tend to notice this pressure—at the same location on their body as it is being exerted—but their dreams are quick to incorporate the stimulus into the sleeping narrative so as to avoid them waking up.[5] It may be as simple as dreaming that one's arm or leg is being held by someone else, or as complex as a sensation of paralysis, or an indeterminate feeling of disequilibrium. What is important is not so much the specific way that the narrative adapts the stimulus to the dream as simply that it does so—demonstrating a synthetic ability to create and sustain a dreamed reality, integrating external stimulus rather than allowing the dream to end.

To conflate these speculative streams—to link the logic of dreams to the experience of digital reality—is to suggest that there is something about how the technological world works that puts pressure on the human imagination. Further, this pressure—like the pressure cuff of dream research—manifests in waking life, most notably through the ways that we quickly integrate elements of digital living into our normal modes of lived experience. In other words, digital stimuli are to waking life what sensory stimuli are to dreams. In my device dream, this was the story of how the Dash captured my imagination with enough force that it put pressure on the dream narrative. It might be thought of as an imprinting of the device upon a human mind. Or, one might think of this relationship as a gesture toward Graham Harman's notion of "vicarious causation," not for its ontological claims but for the importance Harman places on aesthetics (or what he calls "allure") as a way of thinking in a doubled voice (just as a metaphor is literally two things at once, for instance).[6] The pressure is real, but the dream narrative is too—autonomous in the sense that the dream responds to the stimulus with an instinct of self-preservation and sustainability. To think about stimulus causation in dreams as a vicarious process is to insist that a dream incorporates stimuli in ways that are not accountable to the logic of real-world events, and therefore in some way demonstrative of creative independence from this form of logic. In this way, it is possible to avoid an unnecessary competition between the real and the dream and to begin to articulate the basis for an understanding of the ways that dreams are capable of catalyzing sustainable (real) relationships.

More important than the question of causality, however, is the realization that the imagination is permeable to both dreams and the real—an observation that grounds the possibility of thinking about dreams as a form of incorporated speculation. This intensifies the discussion, since it implies that the logic of sleep incorporation is reversible. It is not just dreams that incorporate stimuli drawn from the real world, but reality, too, that sometimes incorporates moments that began while asleep. One might think of the category of dreams where one has a fight with a loved one and wakes up with a lingering anger—a feeling that does not always dissipate right away, and that sometimes persists even after one realizes it was a dream. Sometimes the dream fight in fact causes a real fight. And the same for any of a number of other nightmare-type experiences, in which one falls from a high place, loses one's teeth, is chased or forgets an exam or classroom or conference paper. The result of such dreams is often an abrupt awakening, with a racing heart and sweaty palms—sometimes even a scream—moments where reality incorporates, for a time at least, the residual narrative of the dream itself. And sometimes these moments do not fade, instead becoming actual memories of events that never happened, real memories derived from imaginary sources. In the words of sleep researcher Shelley Adler, an exceptionally distressing episode of sleep "may be of sufficient intensity to elicit symptoms that could be mistaken as an emergent memory of an actual event."[7] A prosthetic memory is born—dreamed into existence. Sometimes these sorts of dreams can even kill, as in the case of Sudden Unexpected Nocturnal Death Syndrome (SUNDS), a rare but real phenomenon involving an otherwise healthy person dying in their sleep.[8]

If one were to theorize this reversibility, it might be termed "reality incorporation," and it might look a lot like a nonreality made somehow, strangely, real. One might place the concept into conversation with François Laruelle's notion of nonphilosophy as that form of engagement that goes straight through the simulation of philosophy to a state of performance, exhausting itself "as an immanent practice rather than as a program."[9] In this case, one might wake up to the real world, but the dream persists; reality incorporates it and thus transforms the dream into a self-fulfilling (performative) reality of sorts, bound to the immanence of the moment rather than to a justification of what counts as dreamed or real. The dream disappears to itself, becomes a nondream in a way that emphasizes that dream incorporation is not just a phenomenon but also a modality of encounter. To propose a form of reality incorporation is to refuse to see dreams as simply a random encounter and instead to take seriously the idea of incorporative logic as a way of understanding a form of illogical causality that yields a more complex interpenetration of cognitive spaces usually thought of as distinct.

Exploding heads

This line of thinking can be made more tangible by referring to the phenomenon known as Exploding Head Syndrome (EHS), an experience that occurs at the edge of dreams, in which one hears a loud explosion in one's head often occurring just as one begins to fall asleep. While deemed clinically harmless, descriptions of the phenomenon note that "by the time the sufferer is wide awake [the sound] is gone, but not surprisingly it leaves in its wake a sense of great consternation and sometimes momentary difficulty in breathing, tachycardia [accelerated heart rate] and sweating."[10] Unlike some instances of dream incorporation that are catalyzed by stimuli derived from outside the mind, there is no known cause for Exploding Head Syndrome. The best theories hypothesize that it occurs as a result of cognitive dissonance between different brain states rubbing against each other as one enters the liminal zone before dreams. And if dream incorporation has a reversible counterpart, why not Exploding Head Syndrome too? Instead of the sound of cognitive dissonance waking one up from hypnagogia, a dream—or something like the beginnings of a dream—erupts into the very reality of the day. And while it may be first recognizable as a racing heart rate or an altered memory or a pronounced ringing in the ears that seems to have come from nowhere, it came, in fact, from the imagination.

If the conflation of dreaming logic and technological living is to be sustained, one might conjecture something like Exploding Head Syndrome as its basis: a sound that emerges from the zone between waking and dreaming minds, to create an effect with real world impact—happening first only as an exceptional instance until the exception becomes the rule and a more ubiquitous version of the syndrome becomes an operational principal for technological reality itself. In other words, a sound that one only knows from a hypnagogic state begins to happen all the time, taking on the momentum of dreams that not only linger, but also begin to spontaneously appear in the world of the everyday. Some of it is the realized science fiction of the world in which we live. Some of it is the unimaginable possibilities that are spoken to us without pause. Some of it is the dizzying accumulation of data drawn from networked technology and its harvested minds—personalities uploaded to the cloud such as to facilitate an even more dream-like existence. What is particularly interesting, however, is that, when contextualized in this sort of metaphoric extension, both dream incorporation and Exploding Head Syndrome translate to much more than dreamtime phenomena. They become new forms of logic that provide a way to conceptualize daytime situations in which memories, fears, and the imagination impact waking reality in real and notable ways. Importantly, to reconceptualize in this way is also to give a social and networked presence to the notion of the dream—no more do our dreams simply come from ourselves, nor would this form of exploding head be limited to the experience of an imaginary crash that wakes one up to the real. Furthermore, the reversibility of incorporative logic demands that the alternate possibility also be true, that the possibility of someone else's dream making a loud crash in the very reality of our daily existence wakes us up to the realization that we are already in the dream itself—someone else's dream in fact.

Jean Baudrillard once called for a "lucidity pact" as a way to position oneself under the sign of a dissipating real. For

Baudrillard this was about fostering a disbelief in reality, lest one be fooled by a simulation that presents itself too convincingly as a brighter, better, newer, and more optimized reality. "Reality: It's to your advantage not to believe in it, since if you believe in it and it doesn't exist, you're duped and swindled and you will die stupid," said Baudrillard, so as to enjoy the possibilities that the simulation has to offer.[11] But then to spin this oneirically—passing beyond lucidity to the technological fabric of dreams—would be to make a pact with exactly the opposite of lucidity, to make a promise not to disbelieve the real but to go along with the dream, choosing the logic of incorporation as the creative agent of delusion itself. It might be to choose to be fooled for as long as the loud sounds of the dream can be made to persist. And indeed this might be just exactly what is required for a world where the devices in my head increasingly tell me more about myself than I can perceive on my own—from my position to my pace, from heart rate to mood, using the very bones of my body to conduct my voice to others, and speaking in ever more collaborative voices directly to the dream that is my reality: a world where dreams refuse to remain in the night and now begin to accompany us technologically in the everyday transactions of performative living.

7

Imaginary magnitudes and the anoriginal hypocrisy that vanishes in the meantime

> *One has to secrete a jelly in which to slip quotations down people's throats—and one always secretes too much jelly.*
> —VIRGINIA WOOLF

Last night I dreamed I had the imagination of a machine. But it was not what I expected. There was nothing cold, nothing calculated about it. No reckonings, no summations. Instead there was a condensation of functions, a displacement of thresholds, & an endless switching of something for nothing. I perceived everything as an exception, as a series of singular events replacing one another according to the laws of chance & coincidence. In effect, I was watching the reality of contingency.

It was like I was dreaming. & my head looked like an apple with a bite taken from it.

When I awoke I had the imagination of a man. But it was not what I expected. A weave of fiber optic cables, copper wires, & electromagnetic radio waves had covered the planet, doubling my neural habits with innumerable subroutines & proliferating data-blooms. What I saw & what I heard in this waking life was striking in its resemblance to my dream: condensed messaging, displaced labor, & the pure ecstasy of communication—of saying so much about absolutely nothing. The world was held together by purchase after purchase & by a manufactured faith in the freedom of choice & absolute need satisfaction.

At first the resemblance to my dream put me in a mood—a sublime panic, to be precise. But then it dawned on me that with dreams above & dreams below, the difference between the hallucinations of animal sleep & the fascinations of technical reverie was moot, or at least largely semantic. I began to grasp that if waking & sleeping had lost their distinction & were now only imaginary magnitudes of the same obscene oneiric activity, then any break between my slumbering-self & waking-I would be expressive not of gaps in reality but of a sliding scale of lucidity.

Mulling this over for a moment, I asked myself how clarity could scale. & then I wondered whether mulling over my mulling something over would be an occasion of more or less clarity. Would a thought about a thought be a more or a less cogent thought? Would a daydream about a dream that I had the night before be a more or a less lucid dream, would its images be more limpid or more turbid? Of course there's no way to tell because both mullings are made of gas—two abstractions containing equal parts flatulence & vapor. In other words, neither thought rises to the heights of meaning nor sinks to the depths of feeling. What the reflective forms of these meditations unleash on experience is an eternity of seduction, lured as they are by the way thought disappears into its own appearances, like the way adjacent mirrors fall into their own reflections, like the way one's voice can vanish in successive copies of itself while sitting in a room, different from the one you are in now.

I suppose treating lucidity as a continuously mutating reflection is like hearing an echo as a sound that perfectly represents its passage through the miscellaneous detours of its milieu. This is how Thoreau thinks about the vale-hopping peals of distant bells that issue from the transports of the Lincoln, Acton, Bedford, & Concord trains. Rather than muddled tolls, he hears a "natural melody" emerge from the bell-tones' passing conversations with every leaf, needle, & bough of the woods. But the irony of this is that the "natural" melody is actually a superbly artificial one, one that retains an expressive fidelity not with its percussive source but with its process of transformation. "Artifice precedes nature." Isn't that what Sartre wrote? Even stranger, however, is that an echo always becomes more than what it was & less than what it will become. Thoreau's echoplex is a paradoxical occasion because its single acoustic event pulls in two directions at once: a referential deformation (bell) & a musical transformation (melody). "All sound is like an echo." Isn't that what Aristotle, who was rumored to have a stutter, once s-s-s-said? Sound is air reflecting its own transformation from one state of agitation to another. It turns out, then, that echoes, too, are made of gas.

Now, what a gas it would be if dreams weren't an echo of waking life but the other way around. Like the melody that finds its way to Walden Pond, I'd think that life's scale of lucidity would depend on how it makes the many dimensions of its carrying-on an active part of its appearance. But the problem that I imagine with this inversion is not a matter of whether life happens multidimensionally or not. The echo shows that a carrying-on always carries on in more ways than one, & its transformation from a mere acoustic occasion to an expressive event indicates that variations are happening to its propagation all at once. However, these various happenings happen with differing degrees of intensity & emphasis that channel perception & desire in ways that make it impossible to express the sense of all these multiple goings-on in a single proposition. So even though Thoreau can hear both the train bells & the melody in the echo, he can only *listen* to one series at a time. He can only make sense of each series one after the other because they both express what eludes the present & causes future & past, more & less, too much & not enough to coincide in the simultaneity of a rebellious matter. The melody-series & bell-series both make sense of what is picked out by the verb "to echo" that specifies each as expressions of its happening.

The problem, therefore, isn't that waking life is insufficiently multidimensional or that it's not weird enough to echo the logical incongruities that typify dreaming life. The problem is that waking life & its excluded middles are a hard-won & hard-to-lose nervous accomplishment that's fated to exclude itself from the very play of all those abstractions that brought it to appearance in the first place. To be conscious, to be "awake" at all, I have to have repressed my species' time in the cradle of condensation & displacement, the time when it discovered that repeating a trauma blunts it & blunting it hallucinates it & hallucinating it is not really experiencing it, & not really experiencing it is, well, thinking it. Although this may have won my kind & me the victory of "thinking" & (for better or worse) our sense of possibility, it also lost us our animal faith & a feeling for destiny. & of the two things to lose, destiny is absolutely the worst, for in its absence we substitute an unlimited experimentation on the given &, as we know, making the given more than given doesn't make the given more given.

But now that I think about it, perhaps this *is* the destiny of that atavistic nervous trick I play on myself over & over again in order to transport the painful impingements of an unqualified real to a more contoured & supple dimension, a dimension that delivers something of myself to remoter affective & symbolic worlds without ever taking me there—actually. What I mean is that this tic is a technique for supplanting the bare activity of something doing with something doing that's exactly not what it appears to be, exactly what it isn't—namely, a thought. & how could I not become addicted to such a psychedelic transport & grow utterly dependent on a physiological ploy that makes an unreal difference that I can actually live through? How could I not be seduced by a semblance that is not what it would be if it wasn't what it is? Why would I not want to dress the world completely in imaginary solutions, adorn the real with what it isn't, & stylize its appearance so that what is felt abstractly becomes more real than the real? Obviously I'm already following the rules of this naturally factitious game, because this sentence is not a sentence, & I am a duck. I suppose, then, that the destiny we lost is the fate of life's becoming more than life, of life becoming a semblance of itself.

But now that I've thought about what I've just thought about, I have the suspicion that the destiny of destiny's neuronal extinction is itself a semblance that my imaginary solutions have raised to the power of paradox. By putting the difference between a gain of thought & a loss of faith in a display of similarity, I'm dramatizing a noncoincidence & effecting a transformation that demonstrates these competing destinies to be modalities of action differentially belonging to the same process of expression. In other words, I'm being ironic. & what is being ironic if not a way of fusing without confusing? Of bringing the sense of what you say & what you don't say together in a single doing? Of performing an action that says what it denies, & denies what it says? Of being yourself & not yourself, like Alice in Wonderland who is always taken as someone else but is never not herself, or an echo, like Alice in Wonderland who is always taken as someone else but is never not herself? Being ironic doesn't first mean being critical; being ironic means being playful, & being playful means multiplying the *value* of an expression to mean this or that by bringing together—in the same act—the excessive ways in which an expression is taken up as meaning this or that.

But thinking again about what I just thought about what I just thought about makes me think that life's many dimensions of carrying-on are most vividly represented (echoed) not by contemplating things but woolgathering them. When I dream or am absentminded, life's multidimensionality becomes *more* apparent, not less. To dream, like "to echo," is to become more than one thing at a time, to elude the present in an infinite identity of both senses at the same time. My wife is my mother, my teeth are my vanity, & I am a rabbit. In a way, the more manifest a difference in a display of similarity is, the more lucid the experience, the more paradoxical, the more playful, the more ludic. Waking life is an echo of a dream's superior irony only when it approaches the lucidity of the latter in its *ludicity*. In other words, life is but a dream when it's absolutely ironic.

I feel that I've heard something like this before. Something about life being a drifting shadow or a confused play told by an idiot whose performers fretfully prance about the stage before they're completely forgotten. I suppose this could be a way of saying that all the world's a stage, or it could be signifying nothing at all. But then again, maybe the world's not a stage but a speaker, always broadcasting its forms & playing parts of itself like a rat flicks its tail or a butterfly dreams. The world could be saying things for the sheer pleasure of exciting the sense that presides over the assignment of the designation of sounds by acting like things without being those things. Oddly, this means that the speaking of the world says what it denies & denies what it says. Like an echo—it's logically undecidable. Like this sentence, which is false. In other words, if all the world's a speaker, then all it has to show are its mediations & the sublime mimesis of its anoriginal hypocrisy.

I wonder, however, if the sublimation of hypocrisy is like daydreaming, which gathers being around its dreamer & gives her the illusion of being more than she is. Does the world assemble itself from what is less-than-being into more-than-being by accumulating & distracting itself with echoes of its mediations? Do these echoes have a link to the elemental energetics of matter that conditions the poetic fidelity & oneiric consistency of daydreaming? If so, does it change things that our material imagination now issues largely from its encounters with the dynamism of technical matter rather than that of earth, water, air, & fire? Are dreams of network pings any different from Emerson's forest-modulated bell-tones? Both exhibit a fidelity to the dynamics of air—visions of reach & extension suffused with images of flight & a yearning to surpass the given. Maybe there's nothing but a stylistic difference between a technical & an organic material, a difference that in this example above leads less to treacly introspective fantasies of renewal & malleability & more to briskly peregrinating visions of promiscuity & contagion.

Perhaps.

But a stylistic difference is a qualitative difference. Style makes a difference as to whether matter's images sing reality or mumble it. Images *sing* when they have a style that abstracts a psychotropic irreality from matter's elemental conduct. & when images sing their drifts & divagations pass between what concentrates being & what exalts it, they animate an awakened oneiricism that resolves into a glimmer of consciousness, a lyrical *cogito*—a wide-awake dreamer. Images stammer if they have no style or poetry, if they denote simply what those elements for which they stand would denote. The concern, then, isn't *that* organic matter differs from technical matter but *how* it differs, how we dream its substance in a way that promotes the feeling of being more than being what is given, a feeling of being absolutely ironic.

& how absolutely ironic it is that I realize the poetry of things only when I find myself too distracted to daydream. The hypocrisy of the world's broadcast that is its creative condition vanishes in the meantime planted in my field of awareness by searching, loading, connecting, connecting, loading, connecting, and loading. Form & function go to seed as one distraction-span distracts another, each digression cultivating not a garden of cares or concerns, but a field of pure transition: Now we are safe... Now you trail away... Now you lag... Now they have all gone... Now the cock crows like a spurt of hard, red water in the white tide... Now we must drop our toys... Now they suck their pens... They wag their tails; they flick their tails; they move through the air in flocks, now this way, now that way, moving all together, now dividing, now coming together... Now the terror is beginning... Now I cannot sink... Now grass & trees... Now the tide sinks... Now my body thaws... Now we are off... Now I hang suspended without attachments. We are nowhere.

Buddha was right: All life *is* buffering.[*]

Now, if anyone is dreaming it's the machines whose incessant & unflagging toil take my capacity to perform an act, to

---

[*] To be precise, it was David who said "all life is buffering," but also (independently) Tom McCarthy, in his novel *Satin Island*.

communicate, to affect, & be affected, as *their* poetic matter. My virtuosity, my potential for producing, for surpassing the given that is my creaturely prerogative has become the material substance of a technical imagination. In other words, *I* am the animal outgrowth that gives machines the psychotropic images, the reveries, the poetry—& maybe even the desire—that qualify their functioning & guide the integrative consilience of their imaginary technics.

If I dream at all, I don't dream that I *have* the imagination of a machine; I dream that I *am* the imagination of a machine. I dream that I'm the oneiric activity & dynamic intoxication of a technical apparatus drunk on the poetry of organic matter's appetite for variation. I'm the dream that dreams the dream that dreams the dream that dreams. In other words, I am a rabbit. Or is it a duck?

Then again, maybe I'm just bluffing …; & if I am, is that not just another form of buffering? Maybe my bells & echoes, melodies & pines, nervous tics, animal spirits, hypocrisies, & reveries are nothing but the troupers of an idiot's play put on to put off the sincerity that their drama would have were they to denote what they would denote. Maybe what I'm saying is exactly what I'm doing: saying the meantime of this event with a single split thinkingness so that the imaginary magnitude of its ludicity & absolute hypocrisy vanishes in the spins & stalls of its own supple semantic spume. Now I pretend again to read. Now glancing this side, that side. Now I am getting the hang of it. Now, without pausing I will begin, on the very lilt of the stroke. Now let me fill my mind with imaginary pictures. Now begins to rise in me the familiar rhythm. Now I sleep; now I wake.

8

We are Lesion

Last night I dreamed that Jack Lemmon was about to conduct a bio-music experiment on me, except he was really Manford Eaton, a cybernetic music investigator whose speculatively audacious proposals—strikingly amenable to control logics—had seized my attention, irresistibly egged on by the apocryphal haze that doggedly stalked his endeavors. We were in the control room of the nuclear plant at the core of the *China Syndrome*, a film depicting a partial meltdown in which Lemmon played a shift supervisor. Uncannily, the thriller was released March 16, 1979, twelve days before a partial meltdown immobilized the Three Mile Island Nuclear Generating Station, near Harrisburg, Pennsylvania, on March 28, 1979. It was an eminently hyperstitional scenario—familiar to our psychedelic times—in which overheated speculation engenders the event itself. Or was it a plagiarism by anticipation? Regardless, the features of "real" and "filmic" analogues were eerily proximate, from the initial indicator glitch that entailed increasingly overcompensatory measures to the media management undertaken after the "accident." Evidence of temporal tampering by occult agents? Who knew?

"Watch for signs of latch-up, ok?"

Lemmoneaton was warning me about the dangers of becoming excessively entrained within the feedback circuit in which I was a key node, my bio-potentials effectively commandeered by an impressive array of sophisticated looking equipment. "A robust loop can overpower the subject, leading to an inability to withdraw, loss of consciousness opening onto … a terminal state."

As Lemmoneaton calmly apprised me of this doom scenario, I took the opportunity to scrutinize him more closely. His face and physical demeanor, though intractably unstable, hovered around a mixture of the genial actor and a heretofore forgotten door-to-door salesman who had unloaded a vacuum cleaner on me, the one I practiced piano with. Having appropriated Glenn Gould's desperate technique of masking the sonorous resultant of physical activity in order to break neurotic feedback loops that frequently threatened to paralyze a performance in its tracks, I could not resist availing myself of this particular appliance for the prodigious noise it expressed. Moreover, Lemmoneaton was speaking in *PAL voice*, unsurprisingly, given that I had just watched the *China Syndrome* in that format. The European standard's temporal resolution—affecting NTSC material with a 4 percent speedup—magically invested him with extra intelligence and authority, his already concatenated insights arriving with an alacrity that gave no quarter.

"Read this." He handed me an untitled sheet of music. It took an extra moment to confirm it was the work of Scriabin; the composer's idiosyncratic notation always temporarily delayed internal listening. The effort had paid off. Lemmoneaton had slyly induced a lucid dreaming state by getting me to read and therefore hear music: it was a failsafe hack, more efficient than staring at my hands had ever been. "Look again," he said. Something was off. It was the beginning of the *Seventh Sonata*, the "White Mass," spliced to its conclusion, the whole piece condensed from twenty-two pages into one. A wormhole. "You're getting it. You need to loosen your sense of time as well as pitch."

He abruptly shifted tone: "These are emissaries from another world where things work differently. The hypermusiac that you are will recognize and appreciate that."

Without warning, "Have You Never Been Mellow" by Olivia Newton-John punctually cut in, just before the first vocal entrance. "It's a control," Lemmoneaton whispered, suddenly beside me. "Such a nice tune. Perfect for establishing your melodic propensities. Pinging your consciousness field to adumbrate your system's history and processing style, ferreting out the concepts that produce the singular habits that grip you. Three words: How. You. Stabilize. Have you never been happy just to hear your song?"

Electrodes were affixed to my scalp, arms, fingers, and chest. Lemmoneaton was back at the controls, adjusting what appeared to be a primitive EEG machine. "Although there exist separate functional systems for perceiving pitch, timbre, rhythm, and so forth, the musical networks of the brain work together in such a way that one parameter of an entity cannot be significantly modified without forcing consequent, ratcheting changes in all the others, soon resulting in the dissolution of musical identity. Impairments to each of these systems yield wildly disparate, unpredictable non-standard musical perceptual syndromes, depending from which parametric position the domino effect is set off."

He added: "This should be amusing."

A strange sensation of being frisked overtook me. It was as if a diagram of melodic curvatures was being synthesized from a repository of tunes stored in my deep memory. I could hear cursory fragments of each in recklessly fast succession. After what seemed like a few minutes, the furtive reconnaissance mission slackened its pace, finally ceding to a monotonous sequence of pitches that I could pinpoint individually—my absolute pitch ability remained intact—yet the rhythmic instability that characterized their arrivals unremittingly suppressed any attempt at assembling them into a melody, abetted by a now inoperative short-term memory, indispensable to the task.

"You're processing signals through an impairment to the right arcuate fasciculus, the tract connecting the auditory and frontal cortices, which I've simulated. You're hearing the resultants of your altered brain scrambling to develop hypotheses to ascertain the contour and direction of the humdrum melody I'm playing back. It's a strange attractor, if you will, acting directly on your newly reorganized virtual. In a sense, you're actively composing what you're hearing now as neural backup systems assemble to pick up the slack. Melodies are keys, emotionally valenced informational bundles, stimulants closely tethered to daily life. Bio-Music is a method for perfecting the channels of emotional communication. The pressure transducers on your fingers are precisely monitoring your affective efforts. The melody is the message."

He paused, as if deliberating on whether to censor himself. "If you want to force a change, set off a crisis." He didn't elaborate.

The experience seemed unreasonably transparent in light of what Lemmoneaton had just disclosed. I was perfectly convinced the music was playing in the room and not in my head, as the output of neural machinations. As I pondered this weird deafspot, the scattered pitches began to magnetize into intervals, monotony slowly giving way to more characteristic articulations, yet a horizon of consistency was still out of reach.

"You know John Archibald Wheeler's doctored Twenty Questions game? The one where, unbeknownst to the subject, the object perpetually morphs as it adapts to the questions, foregrounding the subject's associational matrix while refusing to accumulate into a coherently adumbratable thing? Reality is defined by the questions we put to it. Your planum temporale, the auditory association area exceptionally engorged in your case, is being scanned for schemata, sketchy contour gists that will be applied toward future encounters. Gist-in-time, if you will. If Google Deep Dream isn't yet sonically attuned, it won't be long!" He chuckled.

Lemmoneaton continued, occasionally interrupting himself to pore over numerous readouts. "One of Ben White's experiments at MIT consisted in probing the extent of contour's autonomy as a parameter whose invariance amidst highly mutational procedures—transposed pitches, backwards playback, intervallic stretches—could nevertheless guarantee tune recognition. Being a cartoon junkie, he was abductively inclined towards hijacking the principles of facial caricature to schematize the boundary conditions of melodic cartoon...uh...*contour*. Take a three-dimensional phase-space...*face-space* which diagrammatically includes every conceivable face. Notice how drawing a line from the prototypical, average face at the center through your own face-point towards further vector-coding points yields deformations, caricatures that, paradoxically, more readily conjure your *particular* face."

Lemmoneaton's digression was so provocative that I hadn't noticed the surreptitious insinuation of another melody playing in the background (if indeed it too wasn't a hallucination), which, despite being drenched in reverberation and periodically masked by environmental noise, radiated a curious familiarity.

"This infective air was deployed in a later experiment, circulated by being sung in crowded public spaces. The gambit was straightforward: could ambulatory listeners identify it as a reversed segment from 'Yesterday Once More' by the Carpenters, with none of the artifacts proper to backwards playback as tip off? It was an unusual form of speculative steganophony—hiding in plain hearing—testing whether contour invariance extended to retrograded tunes."

"You remember the game show *Tune Your Speculation*? Three contestants each wrote down a secret melody. The house would generate a semi-random set of pitches that each player then steered, through discrete contour and rhythmic alterations, towards their veiled selection until a member of the audience risked a guess at the liminal edge of emergent familiarity. It was a façade all along, cloaking an experiment tasked with delineating the melodic propensities of a cross-section of folks. It made cybernetic what *Name That Tune* was already doing, in verifying the populace's level of indoctrination and slavish devotion to the latest cultural contrivances. Unfortunately the true nature of the program was leaked, and that was the end of that. Cancelled!"

Indeed, the history of compression, notably pertaining to the MP3 standard, made it abundantly clear that perceptual frameworks could be productively, economically leveraged. Phenomenal real estate lying in wait beyond average human affordances could be and was strategically reallocated to maximize bandwidth profit, all within a tightly regulated cybernetic diagram. What you can't hear you won't miss, the guardians of communicational gateways alleged, basking in the pecuniary promise of newly liberated informational terrain. And it was future-proofed, a self-fulfilling prophecy: if individuals could be trained to listen at lower resolutions, the stage would be set for subsequent abatements, möbiusoidally introduced. A broader question immediately detonated: what models of musical experience could be likewise harnessed, demoting these compression grabs to quaint insignificance?

Lemmoneaton flicked a couple of switches, rote-like. The wandering melody in the foreground gently ceded to a thicker mixture, wet and sludgy, a synthetic composite of uncommonly galvanizing power. Its convulsively variegated patina composed of resonant interference, spatial convolution, and eldritch filtering effectively suppressed melodic recognition. Time was inevitably entangled, its material constitution refusing a steady state, rendering metrical tracking an equally dubious enterprise.

Sporadically, the perceptual load inflicted by this generalized volatility was so debilitating that forward motion thoroughly surrendered, plunging me into breathless contemplation of a timeless, infinitely intricate substance. Despite this surfeit of quicksilver timbral and temporal switching, at least two tunes began to materialize—impossibly—as phantasmal resultants: Marvin Gaye's "Got to Give It Up" and Robin Thicke's "Blurred Lines," strangely fused, were both at issue in the lawsuit I had been investigating. One of the many memoranda fueling this spurious case unfurled a list of "substantial similarities," which required chutzpah to pull off, given that a molecular inspection of these (such as I undertook) could not but defiantly infirm every single one.

Lemmoneaton blurted: "It was a lucky break. Portals are hard to come by. The defendants couldn't have bluffed their way into a multimillion-dollar award all by themselves with a motley array of correlations, each one more gauche than the next. No, their success is symptomatic of dangerously elevated amusial proclivities! But this amusia is not endogenously operated. It's *out there* ..., like Proust's madeleine, which actually contains memory, waiting for the right host to set it free! If anything, our experiment is just extending a process already well under way. People don't really listen to, or even like music. By the way, besides being a timbral palate cleanser—timbrula rasa!—this decoction is also a control, a limiter preventing latch-up."

A long-forgotten dream brusquely overlapped this miasma whose ratcheting contagious effects I could not stave off. I was sitting in the Indie Ale House on a busy night, the clatter and chatter of patrons submerging all but the nether frequencies of the playlist. A bass line slipped into semi-conscious range. It was "Blurred Lines," without a doubt. Being perceptually paranoid, I withdrew discreetly from a conversation to verify this automatic ascription, only to be confronted by "Got to Give It Up." No surprise, the tunes were intertwined in my mind. I checked in with the playback again. This time it was Eddy Grant's "Electric Avenue." Each time I attuned to the background to catch this bait-and-switch red-handed, the tune exchanged on me, like a fugitive virus relentlessly evading capture through cunning counterstrategies. As Justin Timberlake's "FutureSex" took over, White's caricatural diagram flashed in front of me, the four songs and others I could not identify collapsed onto the same vector, extensions of each other. But this was an inaccurate model. The local specifics were of little importance in themselves, the pitiful claims made on their behalf only integumentary smokescreen, occulting the more nebulous contention of affective plagiarism; the domain of *feel* couldn't be colonized outright, likely for fear of ridicule. More charitably, I imagined the defendants deliberately prospecting conflational thresholds, steadily descending into madness, dumbfounded as their allegations of fungibility, each one more extreme than the last, nevertheless always manage to effortlessly secure ratification. In any event, a more judicious representation would account for the nonlinear behavior of song-composites, whose feel could flip on a dime into another state altogether, by infinitesimally nudging one or more variables across a shadowy limit …

Lemmoneaton laughed, rousting me out of the nested reverie. "I do my most catastrophic work in bars."

He pressed on, excitedly. "Of all musical components, timbre requires the most perceptualization, the most neuronal fabrication. Accordingly, it's an accurate transcription of how you *inhabit* hearing, your distortional profile, or how you get things wrong. We're analyzing that now. Timbre's composite effect—spawned by the idiosyncratic summing of diverse waveforms—registers before any determination of cause or origin rushes in to retrospectively corroborate. Neurological spontaneity is truly hallucinatory! The brain speculates wildly, often inappropriately, all the while ablating inconsistencies and rebalancing timbral constituents relative to prior histories. This is why the transforms are swiftly crossfaded rather than hard cut. Lopping off attacks—the fleeting breaks in the sonic continuum—amputates a significant amount of empirical evidence, begetting onset agnosia. Cut the transient, muddle identification!"

Pausing, dramatically: "Chameleons don't become, they change. Amuse-oreille."

Amusia. A generic term for a multitude of what Lemmoneaton dubbed "non-standard musical perceptual syndromes." But there was more to it than met the ear. To amuse is also to deceive. An initiative was undeniably under way—within both the ongoing kaleidophonia and the embedded dream—to dissuade the perceptual apparatus from directly accosting the putative signal. Nothing to hear here. These swapping routines reminded me of Fregoli, the quick-change artist whose name became attached to a delusional belief that different people are one and the same in continuously mutating appearance. Distraction and neglect were paramount conditions for the illusions to fully actualize. The bar songs required a Fregolian affectation to maintain the genericity necessary for background operation. As for the Gaye-Thicke hashwork, I discovered that listening away from it paradoxically remaindered an almost intelligible, trackable (if somewhat ghostly) continuity.

A laptop was now beside me—had it always been there?—on which unfolded in nondescript sound-editing software a torrent of waveforms all overwritten with exquisitely detailed volume curves. Transitions between timbral admixtures were not accomplished through linear abutments, cut-up style, but via machete fades slashing through an absurdly dense thicket of concurrent strata.

"It's the program that generates what you're hearing now, playing out the timbral phase space of these two songs, spectrally and fatally confounded." Lemmoneaton added: "It never ends."

At that moment, another music violently intruded, as if joining a transmission in progress. At least three superimposed layers of staccato rhythmic bursts, running at divergent, but consistent speeds, were tersely organized into Morse-like patterns. Each layer of impulses ferried distinctive material too timbrally obfuscated to make out, though I could periodically discern a couple of voices poking through. It was akin to a procedure I often employed in live improvisation that bound two sonic strata together, one gating the other. An attack of sufficient intensity would open a window endowing the tacit layer with momentary audibility...

Lemmoneaton preempted: "Brute morse! Global metrical alteration incites erratic fluctuations. All lesional anomalies compel awkward reassemblies of noisy stimuli into mutant arrangements in a relativist curvature of the spacetime of behavior. Decidedly true here. It's a decalcomaniacal procedure. Rhythmic grids are imposed onto these songs to repattern beat structures. This'll clean your clock!"

"Metrical perception is an adamantly esoteric construction. A phantom conjuring of something inaudible, virtual into a cogent force. Meter isn't really there, it has to be leeched out. The whole principle of entrainment depends on a co-creative summoning that you're not privy to. Rather, you're granted the impression of a supernatural consonance with a metrical order that seems to obey your central nervous system's cognitive clock without exertion. Tempus fugitaboutit!"

My efforts at extorting a steadfast meter from fraught polyrhythmia, assiduously monitored by Lemmoneaton, subsided as a bivalent stalemate gained the upper hand, a mercurial vacillation between two grooves that occasioned sliding mutations in affective intensity. Moreover, this metrical unresolution precluded any endeavor to compile the manic pulsations into a broader expanse, inhibiting by the same token any engagement in long-term temporal mapping. I felt unhinged.

Furthermore, the extrinsic quality of the music persisted, even though I had been briefed on the extent of my neurological implication in these tests. Faulty indicators were undoubtedly to blame, such as the stuck recorder pen at the origin of the error cascade in the film. Manifold representations hell-bent on enforcing a glassy disinterest in these resolutely occult regimes of percept fabrication. How did I even get this far? In a waking state, my neurological backstage remained decisively inaccessible, happily constrained and overwhelmed by the signals of the outside world, surfacing only in ephemeral moments of maladaptation. Obstinately synthetic, meter is especially susceptible to all manner of primings and cultural conditionings, my particularly Western deafspots perpetuating obliviousness to dimensions that observe fundamentally incompatible logics. Holes upon holes, all the way down.

Lemmoneaton nodded, as if reading my mind: "Transparency is a special form of darkness."

"You know the Black-Scholes-Merton options pricing model in financial speculation, which ended up hyperstitionally ratifying itself into legitimacy, *making reality*? Such is the brain. An engine, not a camera. On becoming deaf, Peirce's friend realized that music needn't involve pressure waves to communicate its charms: 'Now that my hearing is gone I can recognize that I always possessed this mode of consciousness, which I formerly, with other people, mistook for hearing.' His insight led me to the very conceivable notion that music in the future will dispense with sound altogether and become an art of induced psychological, physiological states."

I began to hear Scriabin's "White Mass," which had carried me across the threshold of lucidity at the outset.

"Remember Glenn Gould's multitrack recording experiments replete with microphones deployed from the inside of the piano to the back of the hall? Scriabin wanted to liquidate the world with his *Mysterium*, thankfully unfinished. His eschatological tendencies favored a special kind of parametric anesthesia, radically curtailing harmonic variety to orchestrate an exodus from the expressionism powered by Darwin's categorical affects—what we know as emotions—instead setting traps to lure vitality affects: rushes and withdrawals, explosions and lethargies, transitory movements. Gould wanted to deepen the game, by plotting impossible trajectories and engineering paradoxical sonic realities whose speculative allures seduced him away from the concert stage and its attendant compulsions to steer attention through dramatic time. In his honor, I'm simulating a cingulotomy to maintain you in the phenomenal present. When time binding fails, narrative is obliterated. Any feeling of past-present-future tension vanishes. No more anticipational anxiety or retrospective rumination, just a foregrounding of unassigned affective potential."

Lemmoneaton was on a roll. "My friends in the Television Recuperation Unit were committed neuroformalists. They once superimposed twenty episodes of assorted 70s TV shows selected for the presence of Robert Webber, a self-effacing yet omnipresent character actor, taking advantage of the standard length and structural shibboleths endemic to the drama to foment alchemical transmutations. Excising everything except Webber's image and voice, collapsing parallel realities and temporalities within a single narrative, they made two discoveries. While the overloaded surface giddily traipsed from one non sequitur to another, the legislating powers of form remaindered an undercurrent of sense, cognitively tractable, much like the way the brain stealthily polices perceptual boundaries, ordaining in advance the range of possible experience. Let's face it, all cognition can be exploited because all cognition is bounded. At the same time, this concatenation discharged untold affect, so many weak signals amplified into palpability. Coincidences and déjà vu glitches similarly secrete it on an unusually intensified scale, typical when alternate universes are temporarily juxtaposed. If you regulate a process tightly enough, its meniscus shatters, opening the floodgates to unforeseen contingencies. The more the explicit is codified, the more the tacit can enter into play. It was a TRU maxim. Backdoor aesthetics!"

As he paused, all sound disappeared, exposing my preexisting, albeit heightened tinnitus that began almost instantly fracturing into discrete buzzy tones, gradually forming a melody. Instead of stopping there, it began to infold exponentially, as if in the grip of *horror vacui*. I could tell by his accelerating speech that he knew this was happening.

"White noise research demonstrated how pareidolia becomes a normative condition over long exposures. Passivity is overcome by activity as the mind converts tinnital frequencies to music, establishing dominance. Consider Autonomous Sensory Meridian Response and its touchy-feely molecularities. It wasn't long ago that Argentina's military junta subjected its undesirables to the other ASMR—Ablandamiento Sónico, Modulado por Retroalimentación*—low crackling noises transmitted at unpredictable intervals over headphones, dedicated to dissolving identity. There's a market for that sort of thing now. Don't

---

* Sonic Softening, Modulated via Feedback.

forget McLuhan's observation that art recuperates phenomena obsolesced of their operational usefulness. After all, creativity and paranoia sometimes share the same perception of a surplus of meaning. The brain continuously reimagines what it hears, in an autocatalytic loop, causing neurons in multiple layers of the auditory cortex to fire more and more. Reality only asks to be submitted to hypotheses, so that it can fulfill all of them. Remember how regressive hypnotherapy techniques effectively *precipitated* false memory syndrome? At the end of the day, the brain's will-to-coherence trumps veridicality and induces functional hallucination."

Lemmoneaton had attained the fever pitch of his filmic cognate: "In the future, it is entirely possible for the listener to be transformed by the music whether he wishes to be or not. Conventional music is almost totally helpless to predict and/or control either physiological or psychological states in any very sophisticated manner. The problem of the same physical-sensory stimulation having different effects and meanings to various individuals will eventually be overcome…."

Lemmoneaton interrupted his speech and began scanning the room, muttering. "The signal-to-noise ratio is too low. Schismogenesis!"

As the synthetic melodies ramped up their fractal densification, approaching what I assumed was the feared latch-up, I mulled over the last part of Lemmoneaton's digression. It buttressed a sinking feeling that my neurological propensities were being recruited as co-conspirators in the expansion of control-music schemes, the eccentric oscillations and midway stuck points betraying the true nature of our unwittingly collaborative venture. I had been experiencing affordable, restricted amusia, a cheap knockoff. Though tantalizing, the simulational ploys which I had been exposed to in a lucid state could not be anything but asymptotically inclined. Close but not touching. But even in the grips of pyretic delirium, I couldn't help but appreciate being given access to a perspective—even grossly curtailed—by which perception could be verified, a parallel reality the likes of which had been promised, steadfastly unknowable in waking life.

Without any practicable exchange, musical logics could only fold back on themselves, ingrown fungal excesses proliferating excentrically. It was like the titular China Syndrome. Instead of the exposed core melting down through the bottom of the plant, tunneling its way to the *other side*—China—it hits ground water, blasting into the atmosphere and sending out clouds of radioactivity. Blowback. The sound of false heterogeneity inexorably, desperately prosecuted in the absence of any available ingress to a radically other sensory dimension. Not to mention that the idea of excess itself begged redefinition, so integral was its cooptation by metastatic, perpetually encroaching rationalized exchange. And yet, I knew that alien portals lurked within our world, waiting to be tripped. It was a matter of putting oneself in the way of amusial *deafsides*, by whatever means and on every imaginable perceptual scale. And for that, an as yet unknown set of occult phenomenological tactics had to be devised.

Lemmoneaton threw a second score at me, a single-page compression of Ravel's *Sonatine*, the beginning of the first movement sutured to the end of the Finale. "Read it. Quickly." I did. The excrescences began to thin out toward a manageable quasi-warble. "Backup system. Notational recoding," he said, visibly relieved.

He mopped his brow, catching his breath. "The absolute rule of thought is to return the world as it was given to us: unintelligible. And if possible, to return it a little more unintelligible. A little more enigmatic. The anosognosic hasn't yet learned their lesion." Lemmoneaton bent over and fixated on his coffee cup, which had begun shuddering to a vibration, felt not heard.

CONCLUSION

Attributed to Mercurius 'Scurra (c. 1620).

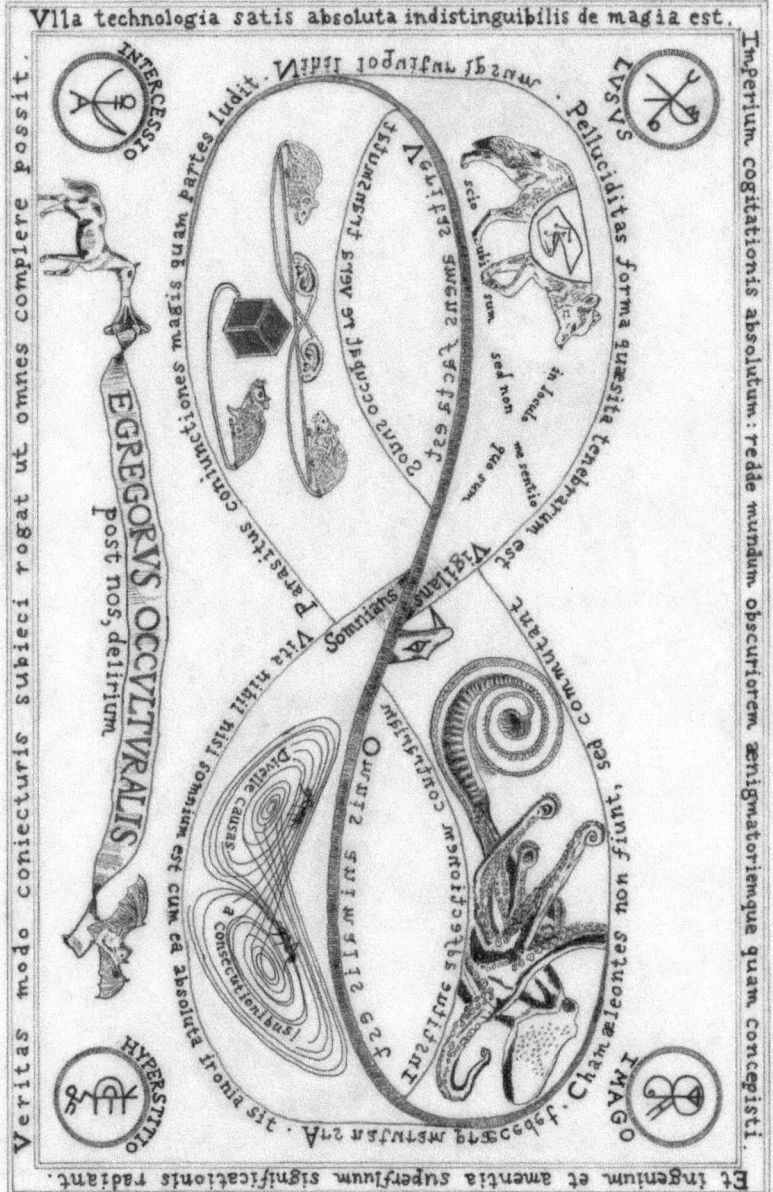

NOTES

Introduction

1 Elizabeth Newton, "The Lossless Self," *The New Inquiry*, September 21, 2015. Available online: http://thenewinquiry.com/essays/the-lossless-self (accessed February 25, 2016).

2 Gilles Deleuze, *Cinema 2: The Time-Image*, trans. Hugh Tomlinson and Robert Galeta (Minneapolis: University of Minnesota Press, 2001), 126–155.

3 Gilles Deleuze, "Capitalism and Schizophrenia," in *Desert Islands and Other Texts 1953–1974*, trans. Mike Taormina (Los Angeles: Semiotext(e), 2004), 262.

4 Delirium ought to be verbified because it connotes an activity of sheer production that's not without sense so much as it is in excess of it. "To deliriate" is thus to make sense of what has too much sense by, paradoxically, making less sense of it.

5 Marshall McLuhan and Bruce Powers, *The Global Village: Transformations in World Life and Media in the 21st Century* (Oxford: Oxford University Press, 1989), 45.

6 Jason Stanyek and Benjamin Piekut, "Deadness: Technologies of the Intermundane," *TDR: The Drama Review* 54, no. 1 (2010): 14–38.

7 Jacques Rancière, *Dissensus: On Politics and Aesthetics*, trans. Steve Corcoran (London: Bloomsbury Publishing, 2010), 149.

8 Massimiliano Gioni, "The Encyclopedic Palace," *55th International Art Exhibition: La Biennale di Venezia* (2013). Available online: http://www.labiennale.org/en/art/archive/55th-exhibition/gioni/ (accessed February 25, 2016).

9 Carl G. Jung, *The Red Book: Liber Novus*, ed. Sonu Shamdasani, trans. Marc Kyburz, John Peck and Sonu Shamdasani (New York: W. W. Norton, 2009), 208.

10 Jonah Lehrer, "Daydream Achiever," *Boston Globe*, August 31, 2008; Josie Glausiusz, "Devoted to Distraction," *Psychology Today* (March/April 2009); Tina Hesman Saey, "You Are Who You Are by Default," *Science News* (July 19, 2009), https://www.sciencenews.org/article/you-are-who-you-are-default; Benjamin Baird et al., "Inspired by Distraction: Mind Wandering Facilitates Creative Incubation," *Psychological Science* 20, no. 10 (2012): 1–6; J. Smallwood et al., "Not All Minds That Wander Are Lost: The Importance of a Balanced Perspective on the Mind-Wandering State," *Frontiers in Psychology* 4 (2013): 441.

11 Recent works such as Reza Negarestani's *Cyclonopedia: Complicity with Anonymous Materials* (Melbourne: re.press, 2008), The Confraternity of Neoflagellants' *thN Lng folk 2go* (New York: Punctum Books, 2013), Stanisław Lem's recently translated *Summa Technologiae* (Minneapolis: University of Minnesota Press, 2013), and Sandy Baldwin's *The Internet Unconscious* (New York: Bloomsbury, 2015) exemplify a tendency to treat fabulation as a form of (post-)critical thought that challenges the posturing of humorlessness as evidence of academic rigor.

12 Mladen Dolar, "The Burrow of Sound," *Differences* 22, no. 2–3 (2011): 129.

13 Gene Youngblood, *Expanded Cinema* (New York: Dutton, 1970), 144.

14 Jean Baudrillard, *The Intelligence of Evil or the Lucidity Pact* (New York: Berg, 2005), 18.

15 Uncertain Commons, *Speculate This!* (Durham; London: Duke University Press, 2013). Available online: http://read.dukeupress.edu/content/9780822376934/9780822376934 (accessed February 25, 2016).

16 Ibid.

Chapter 1

NB: A significant portion of this chapter was developed by copying sections of the essays cited, initially substituting "dreams," "dreaming," and so on, for the various forms of the word computing, and working through the ramifications. These copied sections are sometimes cited and sometimes not, with the choice to do so (or not) being made variously for rhetorical, aesthetic, factual, and fanciful reasons.

1   Mark B. N. Hansen, "Symbolizing Time: Kittler and 21st Century Media," in *Kittler Now: Current Perspectives in Kittler Studies*, eds. S. Sale and L. Salisbury (London: Polity, 2015), 215.

2   Ibid.

3   Ibid., 225.

4   Ibid.

5   Ibid., 226.

6   To be clear, dreams temporalize but this does not exhaust what they are. That is, dreams both take place materially within temporal limitations and at the same time (to the extent they are dreams, and not *just* temporalizations) also exceed those terms through their in-built futurities, anticipations, recollections, absorptions, and recombinations.

7   Cited in Richard Coyne, *The Tuning of Place: Sociable Spaces and Pervasive Digital Media* (Cambridge, MA: MIT Press, 2010), 55–56.

8   Cited in Hansen, 227.

9   Aden Evens, *Sound Ideas: Music, Machines, and Experience* (Minneapolis: University of Minnesota Press, 2005), 1.

10 Mark B. N. Hansen, "New Media," in *Critical Terms for Media Studies*, eds. Mark B. N. Hansen and W. J. T. Mitchell (Chicago: University of Chicago Press, 2010), 180.

11 Briefly, this is problematic because it assumes separability between a sound and its resonance (that is, its sounding contexts).

12 Hansen, "Symbolizing Time," 229.

13 Ibid.

14 Mark B. N. Hansen, *Feed Forward: On the Future of Twenty-First-Century Media* (Chicago: University of Chicago Press, 2015), 80.

15 Ibid.

16 Ibid., 132.

17 Coyne, 56.

18 Hansen, *Feed Forward*, 134.

19 Ted Hiebert, *In Praise of Nonsense: Aesthetics, Uncertainty, and Postmodern Identity* (Montreal: McGill-Queens University Press, 2012).

20 Hansen, "Symbolizing Time," 231.

21 Hansen, *Feed Forward*, 159.

22 Ibid., 80.

Chapter 2

1 Eldritch Priest, "Earworms, Daydreams and Cognitive Capitalism," *Theory, Culture and Society* (forthcoming).

2 Arthur Kroker, *The Will to Technology and the Culture of Nihilism: Heidegger, Nietzsche & Marx* (Toronto: University of Toronto Press, 2004), 74.

3 Dennis Overbye, "Music of the Heavens Turns Out to Sound a Lot Like a B Flat," *The New York Times*, September 16, 2003. Available online: http://www.nytimes.com/2003/09/16/science/music-of-the-heavens-turns-out-to-sound-a-lot-like-a-b-flat.html (accessed February 27, 2016).

4 Robert Krulwich, "Have You Heard about B Flat?" *National Public Radio*, February 16, 2007. Available online: http://www

.npr.org/templates/story/story.php?storyId=7442915 (accessed February 27, 2016).

5   Albert Camus, *The Rebel: An Essay on Man in Revolt* (New York: Doubleday Books, 2012), 6.

6   Ibid., 22.

7   See Sherry Turkle, *Alone Together: Why We Expect More from Technology and Less from Each Other* (New York: Basic Books, 2012).

8   Philip Marchand, *Marshall McLuhan: The Medium and the Messenger: A Biography* (Cambridge: MIT Press, 1998), 281.

9   Ibid., 283.

10 Paul Virilio, *Art and Fear*, trans. Julie Rose (London: Continuum, 2003).

11 Martin Heidegger. *Being & Time*, trans. Joan Stambaugh (Albany: State University of New York Press, 1998), 128.

12 See, for instance, Neurosky's Myndwave headset (http://neurosky.com) or Interaxon's Muse device (http://www.choosemuse.com), both of which offer digitally enhanced meditation experiences.

13 At the time of this writing, the Aurora headset is still in production, with the launch of the product expected in early 2016. More information at: https://iwinks.org/aurora.

Chapter 3

Fifteen steps on how to "speak from the belly"

1   Take a line from Jean Baudrillard. Why? Because who but he could suggest that negative characteristics might be exchanged between humans and machines while at the same time arguing that such an exchange is impossible? See *Impossible Exchange*, trans. Chris Turner (New York: Verso, 2001).

2   Collect a number of passages about "ones" and "counting." One good source is Steven Connor's "'What's one and one and one and one and one and one and one and one and one and one?' Literature, Number and Death" (paper presented at the 20th–21st Literature Seminar, University of Oxford, December 4, 2013), http://stevenconnor.com/oneandone.html; another is his "The Horror of Number: Can Humans Learn to Count?" (paper presented at the University of Toronto, October 1, 2014), http://stevenconnor.com/wp-content/uploads/2014/10/Horror-of-Number.pdf.

3   Invoke something about the relationship between psychotropic drugs and neuroscience. Particularly effective references include the findings that THC produces transient psychotic symptoms in brain regions implicated in schizophrenia, and the clinical evidence that THC impairs certain cognitive processes involved in the inhibition of involuntary responses to various stimuli. More than merely intriguing, this empirical evidence allows us to envision how the brain is more an engine than a camera. See Zerrin Atakan et al.'s "Cannabis Affects People Differently: Inter-Subject Variation in the Psychotogenic Effects of Δ^9-Tetrahydrocannabinol: A Functional Magnetic Resonance Imaging Study with Healthy Volunteers," *Psychological Medicine* 43, no. 6 (2012): 1255–1267. Steven Connor (see above) also borrows findings of Atakan et al. to extrapolate that one of the roles of executive cognitive control is the suppression of what can only be called a compulsion to mean. See his "Panophonia" (paper presented at the Centre Pompidou, February 22, 2012), http://stevenconnor.com/wp-content/uploads/2014/09/panophonia.pdf.

4   Allude to Henri Bergson. For this French philosopher, all forms of life share a capacity to surpass the given insofar as to surpass the given is what counts as "life." Oh yeah—and disregard the circularity of that last bit. So ... see Henri Bergson, *Mind-Energy: Lectures and Essays*, trans. H. Wildon Carr (London: MacMillan, 1920).

5   Remember Gregory Bateson's formulation of the logic of play? Use it liberally. You'll find it in "A Theory of Play and Fantasy," in *Steps to an Ecology of Mind* (New York: Ballantine, 1972), 138–148.

6   Do what Brian Massumi did in *What Animals Teach Us about Politics* (Durham: Duke University Press, 2014)—follow step 5.

7   Always—always!—try to summon the voice of Gilles Deleuze. Most people draw on his work with Felix Guattari. However, if you really want to speak from the belly, go with something from *The Logic of Sense*, trans. Mark Lester (New York: Columbia University Press, 1990).

8   Return to one of your earlier sources. This is Steven Connor again, only this time it's from the paper "Panophonia," mentioned above.

9   Sometimes step 9 is the same as step 8. This is Massumi, but from an earlier work, *Semblance and Event: Activist Philosophy and the Occurrent Arts* (Cambridge, MA: MIT Press, 2011), 145.

10 Step 10 is also step 8 Connor, "Panophonia."

11 Step 11 looks like step 8, but it's actually step 9. Massumi, again from *Semblance and Event*, 152.

12 Make step 11 a final example of step 8. Connor, "Earslips: Of Mishearings and Mondegreens" (paper presented at *Listening In, Feeding Back*, Columbia University, February 14, 2009), http://www.stevenconnor.com/earslips/earslips.pdf).

13 Introduce an obscure thinker, someone like Ernst Cassirer, who argued that perception is not an impassive activity but a proto-symbolic form imbued with *expressive* significance that derives from the affective valence inhering in an event's appearing and being experienced. See his *The Philosophy of Symbolic Forms,* vols. 1–3, trans. Ralph Manheim (New Haven: Yale University Press, 1965).

14 Bring up Susanne Langer. In addition to being both incredibly lucid and insightful, her work exacts an analysis of artworks based not on their formal or medial features but on the experiential effects they compose. It is imperative to mention Langer in this guide to ventriloquy because her concept of "semblance" is a theory of illusion. And what is ventriloquy if not the practice of illusion? See Langer's work *Feeling and Form* (New York: Charles Scribner's

Sons, 1953) for an exhaustive account of the species of illusions that different art forms produce.

15 Repeat step 8. Massumi expanding the purview of Bateson's theory in *Animals*, 5, 22.

Chapter 4

Prompts: Gary Becker, François J. Bonnet, Érik Bordeleau, William S. Burroughs, Roger Caillois, Rob Coley & Dean Lockwood, Cybernetic Culture Research Unit, Matthew Fuller & Andrew Goffey, Donna Haraway, William James, George Kubler, Nick Land, Daniel Levitin, Alexander Luria, Elizabeth Hellmuth Margulis, Declan Morl, Psychosonic Anarchist Detail, Peter Roehr, Danel B. Scroll, Michel Serres.

Chapter 5

1 Steven Connor, "Auscultations" (paper presented at *Sonic Acts XIII: the Poetics of Space*, Amsterdam, February 27, 2010), 10, http://www.stevenconnor.com/auscultations/

2 Ibid.

3 McKenzie Wark, *Telesthesia: Communication, Culture, and Class* (Cambridge; Malden, MA: Polity, 2012), 207–208.

4 Aden Evens, *Sound Ideas: Music, Machines, and Experience* (Minneapolis: University of Minnesota Press, 2005), 6.

5 Eldritch Priest, "Earworms, Daydreams and Cognitive Capitalism," *Theory, Culture and Society* (forthcoming).

6 Benjamin Piekut and Jason Stanyek, "Deadness: Technologies of the Intermundane," *TDR: The Drama Review* 54, no. 1 (2010): 19.

7   Wark, *Telesthesia*, 5.

8   Anna Munster, *An Aesthesia of Networks: Conjunctive Experience in Art and Technology* (Cambridge, MA: MIT Press, 2013), 3.

9   Ibid., 32.

10 James, cited in ibid.

11 Wark, *Telesthesia*, 8.

12 Mark B. N. Hansen, *Feed Forward: On the Future of Twenty-First-Century Media* (Chicago: University of Chicago Press, 2015), 6.

13 For Hansen, the exemplary case of this is Web 2.0, which refocuses "the function of computational media from storage to production, from the archiving of individual experience to the generation of collective presence and of connectivity itself." See Chapter 1 for a deeper dreaming of Hansen's work in these areas. Mark B. N. Hansen, "New Media," in *Critical Terms for Media Studies*, eds. Mark B. N. Hansen and W. J. T. Mitchell (Chicago: University of Chicago Press, 2010), 180.

14 Munster, *An Aesthesia of Networks*, 77.

15 Marc Couroux, "Preemptive Glossary for a Techno-Sonic Control Society," in *Volumes*, eds. Christof Migone and Martin Arnold (Toronto: Blackwood Gallery, 2015), 58–73. Available online: http://xenopraxis.net/MC_technosonicglossary.pdf (accessed March 1, 2016).

16 Ibid.

17 Ibid.

18 W. J. T. Mitchell, "There Are No Visual Media," *Journal of Visual Culture* 4, no. 2 (2005): 262.

19 This fictional example was inspired by the The Listen(n) Project (http://listen.ame.asu.edu/), which I discussed with Garth Paine when it was still in its initial stages of development. However, the example I discuss ultimately bears little resemblance to that project in its actual form.

Chapter 6

1. At the time of this writing, the Bragi Dash is still in production, with the launch of the product expected in early 2016. More information at: http://www.bragi.com.

2. See, for instance, Christian Nold's research on affective and emotional geography (bio-mapping), which uses GSR (galvanic skin response) sensors to chart connections between emotional states and geographic locations. Christian Nold, ed., *Emotional Cartography: Technologies of the Self* (2009). Available online: http://emotionalcartography.net/EmotionalCartography.pdf (accessed March 1, 2016).

3. Arthur Kroker, *Exits to the Posthuman Future* (Cambridge: Polity, 2014), 7–9.

4. Tore Nielsen, "Changes in the Kinesthetic Content of Dreams Following Somatosensory Stimulation of Leg Muscles during REM Sleep," *Dreaming* 3, no. 2 (1993), 99.

5. Ibid., 107–108.

6. Graham Harman, "On Vicarious Causation," in *Collapse: Philosophical Research and Development: Volume II*, eds. Robin James Mackay, Damian Veal and Ray Brassier (Oxford: Urbanomic, 2007), 199.

7. Shelley Adler, *Sleep Paralysis: Night-mares, Nocebos, and the Mind–Body Connection* (New Brunswick: Rutgers University Press, 2011), 68.

8. Ibid., 2.

9. François Laruelle, *The Non-Philosophy Project: Essays by François Laruelle*, eds. Gabriel Alkin and Boris Gunjevic (New York: Telos Press Publishing, 2012), 207.

10. J. M. S. Pearce, "Clinical Features of the Exploding Head Syndrome," *Journal of Neurology, Neurosurgery and Psychiatry* 52 (1989), 909.

11 Jean Baudrillard, *The Intelligence of Evil or the Lucidity Pact*, trans. Chris Turner (New York: Berg, 2005), 156.

Chapter 7

Sources: (in order of appearance)

Jean Baudrillard, *The Ecstasy of Communication*, trans. Bernard Schütze and Caroline Schütze (Los Angeles: Semiotext(e), 2012).

Gilles Deleuze, *The Logic of Sense*, trans. Mark Lester, ed. Constantin V. Boundas (New York: Columbia University Press, 1990).

Brian Massumi, *What Animals Teach Us about Politics* (Durham: Duke University Press, 2014).

Gilles Deleuze and Félix Guattari, *Kafka: Toward a Minor Literature* (Minneapolis: University of Minnesota Press, 1986).

Gaston Bachelard, *The Poetics of Reverie*, trans. Maria Jolas (Boston: Beacon Press, 1969).

China Miéville, *Embassytown* (New York: Del Rey, 2012).

Virginia Woolf, *The Waves* (Cambridge: Cambridge University Press, 2011).

Chapter 8

Prompts: R. Scott Bakker, Jean Baudrillard, Paul Churchland, *le comité invisible*, Manford Eaton, Matthew Fuller and Andrew Goffey, Alexander Galloway and Eugene Thacker, Alexander Gelfand, Glenn Gould, Stefan Helmreich, Maria Hynes and Scott Sharpe, Branden Joseph, Douglas Kahn, Daniel Levitin, Donald McKenzie, Thomas Metzinger and Jennifer Michelle Windt, Anna Munster, Friedrich Nietzsche, Matteo Pasquinelli, Charles Sanders Peirce, Isabelle Peretz, Oliver Sacks, Daniel Stern, Jonathan Sterne, Television Recuperation Unit, René Thom, John Archibald Wheeler, xenaudial.

INDEX

Note: The letter 'n' following locators refers to notes

Ablandamiento Sónico, Modulado por Retroalimentación (ASMR) 137
Absolute ventriloquy 54–5
Adler, Shelly 104
adumbration 57, 123
aesthetics 11, 15, 40, 42, 102–3, 137
Agent Redbreast 89
aliveness 53
  semblance of 83
amusia 13, 129, 132, 139–40
anadumbration 58–61, 65, 70, 78, 80, 123
Aniphonesis 52
Antichrist 31
arcuate fasciculus (right) 125
Aristotle 112
attunement 12, 37–9, 41, 43, 59, 61, 130
audio 12, 23, 53, 90–1, 97
  and reflexivity 98
  and technics 14
augmentation 98
Aurora (device) 42–3
Autonomous Sensory Meridian Response (ASMR) 137

background music 54
B-flat 31, 35, 37, 44
Banks, Hennram 18, 25

Baudrillard, Jean 46, 107–8
Becker, Gary 69
becoming-aphasic 63
becoming-background 78
becoming-musical 65
Being There (film) 58, 78
Benjamin, Walter 41
Bergson, Henri 150n4
Bio-Music (Eaton) 121, 125
black holes 34–5
Black-Scholes-Merton (model) 135
Blurred Lines (Thicke) 129–30
Bragi Dash (device) 97–8, 102
brainwaves 42
buffering (life is) 118–19
butterfly 49. *See also* horse

Cage, John 37, 83
Camus, Albert 36–7
cargo cult 2, 67, 78
Carpenter et al. Downey Lyrical Holdings, a Real-Time Social System, as of March 29, 2007. (Couroux) 76
Carpenters, The 76, 127
Cassirer, Ernst 151n13
China Syndrome, The (film) 121, 123, 139
Chuang Chou 49
cingulotomy 136

compression 71–2, 128, 140
computation 23, 25–8, 71, 88, 94, 99, 152
Connor, Steven 20, 81
Coyne, Richard 25–6
cryptomnesia 65

deafside 140
deafspot 125, 134
Deep Dream (Google) 126
deliriate 3, 145n4
dreams 31, 40–3, 95–6, 100–3, 107–8
    dream incorporation 96, 101, 106–8
    dream-work 4
    dreamed real 19
    lucid dreaming 42
    pressure cuff stimulation 101–2
    REM sleep 101
    sensory basis of 18
    and temporalization 19–20, 147n6
duck 114, 119. *See also* rabbit

earworm 31, 64, 73
    earworm-packets 77
    earworm-spawning 76
Eaton, Manford 121
echo 111–13, 115–16
echoplex 112
egregor (Vodun) 77–8
Electric Avenue (Grant) 130
electronic culture 38–9, 41–4, 96–100, 102, 106–8
Electronic Voice Phenomena 69
entrainment 41, 62, 64, 77, 133
Exploding Head Syndrome 96, 105–6

face-space 126
Fourier analysis 23–8
Fregoli, Leopoldo 132
FutureSex (Timberlake) 130

gating 133
Gaye, Marvin 129, 132
Gibson, William 43
Gnossienne #5 (Satie) 58
Gnossienne #6 (Satie) 58, 80
Got to Give It Up (Gaye) 129–30
Gould, Glenn 89, 122, 135
Grant, Eddy 130

hallucination 3, 7–8, 50, 52, 69, 74, 110, 113, 127, 131, 138
Hamlet 52
Hanker, Mans 18–19, 27
Hansen, Mark 23–8, 88, 147–8, 152
Harman, Graham 102
Heidegger, Martin 39–41
Hiebert, Ted 26
horse (as non-horse) 49. *See also* butterfly
hypermnesia 57–8
hypermusia 123
hyperstition 56, 66–71, 78–9, 135
    functionality 69
    gambit 68
    scenario 121
hypnagogia 106

imagination 7, 13, 40, 43, 96–7, 102–3, 107, 117, 119
Inception (film) 64
infra-legibility 58

INDEX

irony 52, 55
   dream's superior form of 116
   truth of 56

James, William 70, 77, 80, 88
Joel, Billy 74
John, Elton 74

Kahn, Man Res 18, 19
kaleidophonia 132
Kapital Verinnerlicht (Anonymus) 61
Kittler, Friedrich 21–3, 28, 47
Kroker, Arthur 31–3, 98–100
Kubler, George 70

Langer, Susanne 151n14
Laruelle, François 104
Lemmon, Jack 80, 121
listening 2, 5, 52, 64–5, 81–7
   away 2, 5, 132
   internally 58, 123
   purview of 6
loop-effect 58
ludicity 116, 119
Luria, Alexander 57

Maenz, Paul 62
Mandel, Johnny 58, 80
McCarthy, Tom 118
McLuhan, Marshall 40–2, 109–10, 138
melody 63, 81, 111–13, 124–8, 137
meter 133–4
microtemporality 24–6
Mitchell, W.J.T., 91–2
Morl, Declan 67–70

motivation 95, 97
movement-network 62–5
Munster, Anna 87–8
Muzak 75

Name That Tune (game show) 127
NASA 34–6
Nebenformeln (Scroll) 73–4
neuroformalism 136
Newton-John, Olivia 123
Nietzsche, Friedrich 1–2, 12, 31–3, 35, 37–8, 43–4

Orbison, Roy 47
oto-acoustic 82, 85

Paine, Garth 91
PAL voice 122
Pareidolatry (Morl) 67, 70
pareidolia 72, 137
'pataphysics 12, 31, 95, 97
Peirce, C.S., 135
Pessoa, Fernando 46
phonochasm 89–92, 94
phonocollapse 89–91
planum temporale 126
poetic fidelity 117
Priest, Eldritch 31
psychasthenia 79
Psychosonic Anarchist Detail 75

Queen, White 47

Rabbit 115, 119
Raudive, Konstantīns 69
Reagan, Ronald 69

repetition 31–4, 37, 60–1, 63–5, 71–3
revalencing machine 70
Roehr, Peter 61–5, 68, 71–2

S (Solomon Shereshevsky) 57–60, 65, 79
Sartre, Jean-Paul 111
Satie, Erik 58, 80
Scriabin, Alexander 123, 135
Scroll, Danel B., 61, 71–5, 80
'Scurra, Mercurius 142
Sellers, Peter 78–9
semantic satiation 63
semantic spume 119
servitor (Vodun) 62
Shazam (app) 75
silence 36–7, 46, 48, 97
simulation 12, 23, 92, 108, 139
Sonatine (Ravel) 140
sonic branding 59–60, 74
speculation 34, 38–40
    financial 135
    incorporated 103
steganophony 127
Sudden Unexpected Nocturnal Death Syndrome (SUNDS) 104

teleplasty 78
Television Recuperation Unit (TRU) 136
templex 59, 70, 72

Temporal finitude, law of 18–19, 24
texture 84–5, 87, 89, 92
Thicke, Robin 129, 132
Thoreau, Henry David 111–12
Timberlake, Justin 130
timbre 124, 131
time and motion studies 71
time-binding 60, 63–5, 79, 136
tinnitus 13, 81–2, 94, 137
Tune Your Speculation (game show) 127
Turkle, Sherry 38

Valéry, Paul 71
value (play) 115
vampire effect 74
vector 5, 12, 65, 72, 82, 84–5, 91, 94, 126, 130
Virilio, Paul 40

Wallace, David Foster 54
Wark, McKenzie 88
Webber, Robert 136
Wheeler, John Archibald 126
White, Benjamin 126
White Mass (Seventh Piano Sonata) (Scriabin) 123, 135
Woolf, Virginia 109

Yesterday Once More (The Carpenters) 127

www.ingramcontent.com/pod-product-compliance
Lightning Source LLC
Chambersburg PA
CBHW070333230426
43663CB00011B/2296